General editor: Graham Handley MA PhD

Brodie's Notes on William Shakespeare's

The Taming of the Shrew

T. W. Smith BA

Former English master, Barrow and Teignmouth Grammar Schools

Pan Books London and Sydney

This revised edition published 1986 by Pan Books Ltd,
Cavaye Place, London SW10 9PG
9 8 7 6 5 4 3 2 1

ISBN 0 330 50226 3
Photoset by Parker Typesetting Service, Leicester
Printed and bound in Great Britain by
Richard Clay (The Chaucer Press) Ltd, Bungay, Suffolk

Other titles by T. W. Smith in the Brodie's Notes series:
Henry V
Love's Labour's Lost
Julius Caesar
A Midsummer Night's Dream
The Tempest

Contents

Line references in these Notes are to the *Arden Shakespeare: The Taming of the Shrew*, but as references are also given to particular acts and scenes, the Notes may be used with any edition of the play.

Preface

This student revision aid is based on the principle that in any close examination of Shakespeare's plays 'the text's the thing'. Seeing a performance, or listening to a tape or record of a performance, is essential and is in itself a valuable and stimulating experience in understanding and appreciation. However, a real evaluation of Shakespeare's greatness, of his universality and of the nature of his literary and dramatic art, can only be achieved by constant application to the texts of the plays themselves. These revised editions of Brodie's Notes are intended to supplement that process through detailed critical commentary.

The first aim of each book is to fix the whole play in the reader's mind by providing a concise summary of the plot, relating it back, where appropriate, to its source or sources. Subsequently the book provides a summary of each scene, followed by *critical comments*. These may convey its importance in the dramatic structure of the play, creation of atmosphere, indication of character development, significance of figurative language etc., and they will also explain or paraphrase difficult words or phrases and identify meaningful references. At the end of each act revision questions are set to test the student's specific and broad understanding and appreciation of the play.

An extended critical commentary follows this scene by scene analysis. This embraces such major elements as characterization, imagery, the use of blank verse and prose, soliloquies and other aspects of the play which the editor considers need close attention. The paramount aim is to send the reader back to the text. The book concludes with a series of revision questions which require a detailed knowledge of the play; the first of these has notes by the editor of what *might* be included in a written answer. The intention is to stimulate and to guide; the whole emphasis of this commentary is to encourage the student's *involvement* in the play, to develop disciplined critical responses and thus promote personal enrichment through the imaginative experience of our greatest writer.

Graham Handley

Shakespeare and the Elizabethan Playhouse

William Shakespeare was born in Stratford-upon-Avon in 1564, and there are reasons to suppose that he came from a relatively prosperous family. He was probably educated at Stratford Grammar School and, at the age of eighteen, married Anne Hathaway, who was twenty-six. They had three children, a girl born shortly after their marriage, followed by twins in 1585 (the boy died in 1596). It seems likely that Shakespeare left for London shortly after a company of travelling players had visited Stratford in 1585, for by 1592 – according to the jealous testimony of one of his fellow-writers, Robert Greene – he was certainly making his way both as actor and dramatist. The theatres were closed because of the plague in 1593; when they reopened Shakespeare worked with the Lord Chamberlain's men, later the King's men, and became a shareholder in each of the two theatres with which he was most closely associated, the Globe and the Blackfriars. He later purchased New Place, a considerable property in his home town of Stratford, to which he retired in 1611; there he entertained his great contemporary Ben Jonson (1572–1637) and the poet Michael Drayton (1563–1631). An astute businessman, Shakespeare lived comfortably in the town until his death in 1616.

This is a very brief outline of the life of our greatest writer, for little more can be said of him with certainty, though the plays – and poems – are living witness to the wisdom, humanity and many-faceted nature of the man. He was both popular and successful as a dramatist, perhaps less so as an actor. He probably began work as a dramatist in the late 1580s, by collaborating with other playwrights and adapting old plays, and by 1598 Francis Meres was paying tribute to his excellence in both comedy and tragedy. His first original play was probably *Love's Labour's Lost* (1590) and while the theatres were closed during the plague he wrote his narrative poems *Venus and Adonis* (1593) and *The Rape of Lucrece* (1594). The sonnets were almost certainly written in the 1590s though not published until 1609; the first 126 are addressed to a young man who was his friend and patron, while the rest are concerned with the 'dark lady'.

The dating of Shakespeare's plays has exercised scholars ever since the publication of the First Folio (1623), which listed them as comedies, histories and tragedies. It seems more important to look at them chronologically as far as possible, in order to trace Shakespeare's considerable development as a dramatist. The first period, say to the middle of the 1590s, included such plays as *Love's Labour's Lost, The Comedy of Errors, Richard III, The Taming of the Shrew, Romeo and Juliet* and *Richard II*. These early plays embrace the categories listed in the First Folio, so that Shakespeare the craftsman is evident in his capacity for variety of subject and treatment. The next phase includes *A Midsummer Night's Dream, The Merchant of Venice, Henry IV Parts 1 and 2, Henry V* and *Much Ado About Nothing*, as well as *Julius Caesar, As You Like It* and *Twelfth Night*. These are followed, in the early years of the century, by his great tragic period: *Hamlet, Othello, King Lear* and *Macbeth*, with *Antony and Cleopatra* and *Coriolanus* belonging to 1607–09. The final phase embraces the romances (1610–13), *Cymbeline, The Tempest* and *The Winter's Tale* and the historical play *Henry VIII*.

Each of these revision aids will place the individual text under examination in the chronology of the remarkable dramatic output that spanned twenty years from the early 1590s to about 1613. The practical theatre for which Shakespeare wrote and acted derived from the inn courtyards in which performances had taken place, the few playhouses in his day being modelled on their structure. They were circular or hexagonal in shape, allowing the balconies and boxes around the walls full view of the stage. This large stage, which had no scenery, jutted out into the pit, the most extensive part of the theatre, where the poorer people – the 'groundlings' – stood. There was no roof (though the Blackfriars, used from 1608 onwards, was an indoor theatre) and thus bad weather meant no performance. Certain plays were acted at court, and these private performances normally marked some special occasion. Costumes, often rich ones, were used, and music was a common feature, with musicians on or under the stage; this sometimes had additional features, for example a trapdoor to facilitate the entry of a ghost. Women were barred by law from appearing on stage, and all female parts were played by boy actors; this undoubtedly explains the many instances in Shakespeare where a woman has to conceal her identity by disguising

herself as a man, e.g. Rosalind in *As You Like It*, Viola in *Twelfth Night*.

Shakespeare and his contemporaries often adapted their plays from sources in history and literature, extending an incident or a myth or creating a dramatic narrative from known facts. They were always aware of their own audiences, and frequently included topical references, sometimes of a satirical flavour, which would appeal to – and be understood by – the groundlings as well as their wealthier patrons who occupied the boxes. Shakespeare obviously learned much from his fellow dramatists and actors, being on good terms with many of them. Ben Jonson paid generous tribute to him in the lines prefaced to the First Folio of Shakespeare's plays:

Thou art a monument without a tomb,
And art alive still, while thy book doth live
And we have wits to read, and praise to give.

Among his contemporaries were Thomas Kyd (1558–94) and Christopher Marlowe (1564–93). Kyd wrote *The Spanish Tragedy*, the revenge motif here foreshadowing the much more sophisticated treatment evident in *Hamlet*, while Marlowe evolved the 'mighty line' of blank verse, a combination of natural speech and elevated poetry. The quality and variety of Shakespeare's blank verse owes something to the innovatory brilliance of Marlowe but carries the stamp of individuality, richness of association, technical virtuosity and, above all, the genius of imaginative power.

The texts of Shakespeare's plays are still rich sources for scholars, and the editors of these revision aids have used the Arden editions of Shakespeare, which are regarded as pre-eminent for their scholarly approach. They are strongly recommended for advanced students, but other editions, like The New Penguin Shakespeare, The New Swan, The Signet are all good annotated editions currently available. A reading list of selected reliable works on the play being studied is provided at the end of each commentary and students are advised to turn to these as their interest in the play deepens.

Literary terms used in these notes

Alliteration The repetition of initial consonants close together: 'leave and leisure' (I,2,135); 'as peremptory as she proud-minded' (II,1,131). For emphasis or merely a jingle.

Analogy The use of a similar action or situation as an illustration (looser than a simile): Petruchio compares his taming of Katherina to the training of a falcon; or fine clothes to a jay's feathers (IV,3,172).

Hyperbole Intentional exaggeration for effect and not to deceive. There are several instances typical of a play marked by extravagant behaviour: Biondello's portrait of the approaching bridegroom (who has to appear on the stage) is far exceeded by that of his horse (who has only to be imagined); Petruchio's promise of gay apparel (IV,3,55–60) is a scornful attack on fashionable 'knavery', soon given substance in his truly hyperbolical condemnation of the elaborate costume executed to his own order.

Irony Expressing the opposite of what is really meant: Kate's description of Baptista's marrying her off to Petruchio as 'a tender fatherly regard' (II,1,279); after listening to the plan to deceive Baptista, the caustic Grumio comments, 'Here's no knavery!'

Pun The bringing together of two words with the same (or nearly the same) sound, but different meanings; usually intended as a joke, it has been called 'the lowest form of wit'. There are varieties among those perpetrated in this play.

Two meanings of the same word: 'base' in character and the musical 'base', now spelt 'bass' from the Italian 'basso' (III,1,45).

Two homophones (same pronunciation with different spelling): 'ring' and 'wring' (I,2,16).

An earlier vowel sound has to be understood: 'heard' as 'hard' (II,1,183).

The two sounds may be only approximate: 'stoics' and 'stocks' (I,1,31).

A root word and its derivative with a prefix: 'figure' and 'disfigure' (I,2,112).

Grumio achieves a double pun: 'countenance' with 'face' and 'credit' (IV,1,88–94).

Blank Verse The bulk of Shakespeare's dialogue, as well as major poems by our chief poets, is composed in *decasyllabic* lines (of ten syllables) with no end-rhymes, hence the term 'blank'. The scansion is predominantly *iambic* (bearing the spoken stress on the second syllable of each of the five 'feet'). The absence of rhyme and some variation in the placing of the stresses enable this metre to approximate to normal speech while conveying by its rhythm more emotion than prose. Decasyllabic verse is also rhymed, usually in pairs of lines called *couplets*, but also in *quatrains* (four-line stanzas). Most scenes in this play end in a rhyming couplet to indicate the break in the action.

The play

Plot

Baptista, wealthy citizen of Padua, has two daughters of opposite temperaments. The story of their courtship and their unusual weddings (one in great haste, the other in extreme secrecy) forms the framework of the play. Bianca, the younger of the two, is beset by suitors whose intrigues provide the action of the sub-plot. Her father's refusal to allow further courtship until her shrewish elder sister is married is the cause of the main plot. Until the Shrew is tamed, no marriage can take place.

Baptista looks for tutors to keep his favourite Bianca occupied, while the suitors look round for a husband for Katherina. Two new arrivals in Padua are Lucentio, who falls romantically in love with Bianca, and Petruchio, who rather cynically is prepared to marry anyone for money, though he has plenty. Lucentio obtains access to Bianca disguised as a tutor; Petruchio wins a rowdy battle of wits with Katherina and dictates a wedding-day (agreed to gladly by her father).

Even more surprising is the shabby appearance of the bridegroom, his disorderly conduct at the wedding, and the abandonment of the wedding feast for a wild ride through atrocious weather to his home, where the bride is brow-beaten, starved and tormented into submission. Meanwhile Lucentio has instructed his manservant Tranio to confuse the other suitors by pretending to pay court to Bianca in the person of his master; this would also draw Baptista's attention away from Lucentio, who is planning a runaway marriage. Tranio, having as 'Lucentio' outbid the wealthy Gremio for Bianca's hand, persuades another arrival in the town, a Pedant, to stand in as his father (i.e. the father of the real Lucentio) and guarantee the enormous dowry he has offered. Where Petruchio has stormed his way in to fetch his bride, Lucentio slips quietly across the threshold for a second, though more decorous, marriage off-stage.

Vincentio, father of Lucentio, now arrives, is encountered by Petruchio and Katherina returning to the town and brought to his son's apartments, where, to his surprise, he is greeted as an impostor. When all is explained by the appearance of Lucentio and Bianca together, the two offended parents are not easily mollified. Looking on with much amusement are the Shrew and her Tamer, whose mutual respect has developed into a harmonious relationship – a contrast with the lack of confidence in each other shown now by the romantic pair in the concluding banquet scene. Katherina's implicit obedience to her husband's least (or most outrageous) request is demonstrated, and her wifely duty defined in a long concluding speech. The serenity of her mood elevates her in the view of her hearers to a position equal if not superior to that of her lord and master.

The Induction

The above comedy is represented as being performed by travelling players in a lord's house as part of the entertainment he has laid on for the reception and mystification of a drunken tinker, picked up outside a tavern and transferred to a life of luxury, apparently as an experiment in psychology to see how far the abrupt change would be accepted by a man in his circumstances. This idea, however, seems to have evaporated after the two opening scenes, as the play gathered momentum and shed its earlier worldliness for higher flights of character contrast, in which real love is engendered. Though Sly the Tinker has become one of the favourite characters in Shakespeare's gallery, we do not really wish to be reminded of his existence nor to see him torn from his 'wife' and returned to the gutter.

Sources

Nearly all of Shakespeare's plots can be traced, with varying degrees of certainty, to their sources. He borrowed freely from contemporary fiction, translations and histories, transforming what he took into something fuller and richer. He must have been an omnivorous reader, with a retentive memory, and no doubt he listened to much absorbing talk about public affairs and foreign travel. Much material would be used as it crossed his mind, often with an aptness of expression which has made it immortal.

His works have long been a mine for researchers looking for allusions, archaic words, folklore, personal references, even coded messages for posterity! *The Taming of the Shrew*, most unpoetical of his comedies, has an unexpected number of classical and other allusions. Particularly interesting is the use of the

Roman poet, Ovid; he is recommended to Lucentio as pleasant alternative reading to Aristotle; he is studied with Bianca, though the extract so cunningly mistranslated comes from an Epistle in the *Heroides*, not *de Arte Amatoria.*

Among Shakespeare's predecessors was George Gascoigne (1525–77), who is credited with the first English comedy in prose (he was also a pioneer of the blank verse used throughout Shakespeare's plays). *The Supposes* (acted 1566) was largely a translation of *Gli Suppositi* (1509) by the famous Italian, Ludovico Ariosto. The 'supposes' meant 'fraudulent substitutes', a meaning kept by 'supposition' until the 18th century. They find an echo in 'suppos'd Lucentio' (II,1,401) and 'counterfeit supposes' (V,1,107). A comparison shows how much was borrowed: Lucentio's instant love, the exchange with Tranio, the latter becoming a suitor, the auction by Baptista, the need of a father to guarantee the contract, the Pedant frightened by a pretended war into giving the guarantee, the confrontation of real and supposed fathers, Tranio's extraordinary refusal to recognize his old master. But in *The Supposes* Bianca has no sister. In our play the relationship links this sub-plot with the main plot, to which similarities have been found in *The Taming of a Shrew* (not *the* Shrew), a crude play published in 1594. The name of the Shrew is Kate, but her tamer is Ferando. There is nothing of our sub-plot, but Kate has *two* sisters. Some features are so close a parallel that this old play has been regarded as a first version by Shakespeare, later improved and added to by him at a maturer stage in his career. It contains the mad wedding, the tantalizing of Kate with offers of food, the treatment of the tailor, the sun-and-moon dispute, and the pretence that the old merchant is a young lady. Most of all it has the Induction *complete*, with Sly's comments at intervals. Did Shakespeare forget the rest of the Induction or quietly drop it?

Treatment

Various conjectures have been made as to how much of the play is Shakespeare's work and how much that of some predecessor or collaborator; attention has been drawn to the general superiority in substance and style of the main plot over the sub-plot. The scenes involving Katherina on the one hand and Bianca on the other mostly alternate, and the two plots could be separated without great difficulty; the result, however, would be half a play in each case, shorn of contrasts (see the section on

Structure). Considering the great disparity to be found in Shakespeare's drama as a whole, from profoundest tragedy to the emptiest farce, and recognizing that there is little likelihood of our ever being able to discriminate definitely between what he wrote and the contributions of others, it is wiser to accept *The Taming of the Shrew* as his entirely, produced sometime between 1594 and 1597. We might guess that, under pressure when the theatres were reopened after the plague-year of 1593, he saved time by combining his own script of the taming plot with another's version of the intriguing plot, with minor adjustments, as well as some incongruities caused by securing a general reconciliation before the final exit. There is the same boisterous spirit and rough horse-play in *The Merry Wives of Windsor*, written at about the same time, in which the role of the sexes is inverted – it is the male who is humiliated (demonstrating what is today admired as 'impartiality'). In both plays incidents like the tipping of the famous laundry-basket into the Thames and Katherina's wedding ceremony have to be imagined as happening off-stage. And, when drafting the fate of Hortensio, did Shakespeare have in mind the widow whom Gascoigne, author of *The Supposes*, was driven by circumstances to marry?

There is, therefore, no need to think of Shakespeare as having invented this extravagant story, nor, indeed, of his having adopted it as a dramatic illustration of *how* to tame a 'shrew', a word (peculiar to the English language) employed for the kind of virago who used to be strapped to a 'ducking-stool' and briefly immersed in the village pond (a custom largely confined to this country). Itself the product of some primitive superstition, the term was originally applied to members of either sex; for some reason, it came to be limited to female scolds. Shakespeare may have, as in the case of Falstaff, tipped the balance more than a little, but he remains free of the charge of malicious bias. As was his custom, he took another's piece of fiction, with its arresting title, and, rather hastily, infused it with a measure of his understanding of genuine human character, especially the characters of young heroines. There is no kind of moral, only the subtle arousing of sympathy among the spectators for a spirited girl put through the whole 'gamut' of psychological warfare!

Text

The play as we know it was first published in the Folio edition of 1623, seven years after the death of its author. It is one of eighteen that had not, as far as we know, appeared in print before. Others had been published as single plays in quarto form (sixpence each, as against one pound for the folio) and these, whether good or bad or pirated, help to date the titles concerned. Though Heminge and Condell, the two editors, used the best copies in manuscript or print they could find, the compositors had their fair share of human error, and even the proof-reading seems to have been done with an eye to type-correctness and little reference to the copy itself. Miscalculations in paging meant that sometimes verse was set down as prose to save space, or prose arranged as verse to fill in. Hence the impossibility of establishing a standard numbering of lines.

As we have seen, quartos were cheaper and more profitable; the Folio, a financial risk, was a monument to the poet by his friends. When we consider the limited ideas on copyright in that age, how manuscripts were bandied about as prompt copies and were often the property of the acting company, so that many failed to be printed and, therefore, perished, we may well be content that one more comedy, with all its imperfections and crudities, has survived to entertain us with an old fable transformed.

Scene summaries, critical commentaries, textual notes and revision questions

Induction Scene 1

After a violent argument with an ale-wife (identified in the following scene as Marian Hacket of Wincot, a few miles south of Stratford) Christopher Sly, tinker by trade, falls into a drunken stupor. A neighbouring lord, returning home with his huntsmen, comes across the unconscious form lying in a grotesque heap in the road and has the sudden impulse to take him to his mansion, put him to bed in luxurious surroundings and set his household to wait on him with delicious food. The huntsmen are given instructions about the preparation of the room, the music to be played, the scented water and the towel, the rich clothes to be put on (as if to satisfy the most exquisite taste); they are to explain to the tinker that he is really a powerful lord who has been out of his mind for fifteen years, to the great sorrow of his lady and the household.

Trumpets announce the approach of a band of players, who propose to visit the lord and hope for accommodation in return for their entertainment. They are immediately drafted into the conspiracy as part of Sly's 'dream', but are warned not to break out into open laughter at the odd behaviour of the 'lord' before whom they are to perform.

Then the lord sends a serving-man to his page, Bartholomew, with orders to dress up as Sly's lady and come to him in tears of gratitude for his 'recovery'.

Commentary

Sly has smashed the hostess's glasses with as much abandon as Petruchio later hurls his own tableware at the servers. There is, however, no reason to see in this whole episode some deliberate social observation by Shakespeare; the theme is change, especially the changing moods of human nature, brought about by tricks, some long prepared, others on the spur of the moment. We see this play, full of tricks, introduced by the pursuit of a spontaneous lordly whim, the object of which is to see whether such a humble and fuddled member of society can be made to accept his transformation. If he woke up in a four-poster, would he forget who he was? As transformation of character, from shrew to model wife, is to be the subject of the play itself, this transformation from poverty to affluence can be regarded as something of a 'curtain-raiser'.

In contrast with the stern contemporary treatment of vagrants this local English squire offers luxurious accommodation for the unconscious tinker, but only as a jest, or perhaps, in the spirit of the age, as an experiment (like Sir Francis Bacon's fatal decision, on a wintry day, to try stuffing a dead fowl with snow to preserve the meat). Sly's resultant behaviour was to be a 'pastime' for the (controlled) amusement of all who beheld it, a milder form of the contemporary forms of baiting; it is to be noted that the hunting party was returning without any animal trophies – perhaps in his disappointment the lord found compensating prey in the 'simple peasant'. His carefully planned resuscitation of a dead drunk into one leading a completely other-world existence is as fantastic as the wild wooing which Petruchio is to 'practise' on his shrew. The lord's 'sport' is developed further in the sudden impulse to supply typical entertainment in a stately household, to drive away the imagined melancholy with a players' performance full of 'mirth and merriment'.

Like Hamlet, this lord is a follower of theatricals; he even ventures independently of the players on a device of his own to add to the pleasure of the victim; in so doing he provides a remarkable description of an imaginary performance by a boy actor of the day playing an emotional woman's part. Whether this particular page, thus suddenly called upon, had had occasion to take such a part in some previous local pageant, we can only guess; there is a contrast with the newly arrived professionals in the reference to the amateur's resource of the tear-jerking onion! And the lord seems to have full confidence in the page's ability (he is there to learn courteous behaviour by example) to copy the actions of dutiful spouses displaying their affection to their lords – the conversion to which beatific state from headstrong wilfulness is to be the subject of the day's entertainment.

feeze Beat.
the chronicles Shakespeare drew much material for his plays from

Holinshed's *Chronicles*, first published in 1577.

we came in with Richard Conqueror Our ancestors 'go back to the Normans'. The tinker confused Richard 'Lionheart' with William 'the Conqueror'.

paucas pallabris Mispronunciation of *pocas palabras*, Spanish for 'few words'.

Sessa! Possibly a similar mispronunciation of Spanish *cese*, imperative of *cesar*, to stop doing something, e.g. talking. Rather like using 'Cease!' instead of 'Shut up!'

denier A small French copper coin.

Go by, Saint Jeronimy A popular comic phrase, in the sense of 'Vanish!', based on a line in *The Spanish Tragedy*, by Thomas Kyd, produced in 1594. The hero is Hieronimo (Jeronimo). If the Folio is correct with 'Go, by St Jeronimy', Sly must be supposed to have confused this name with St Jerome, whose order of hermits were called 'Jeronomites'.

thirdborough Elizabethan term for 'constable'. Possibly a corruption of 'fridborgh', a peace-warrant. Sly makes play with 'third'.

kindly (Act) according to his kind. Spoken sarcastically.

emboss'd Foaming at the mouth.

couple Leash together.

brach Bitch.

in the coldest fault With the scent lost and gone quite cold.

cried . . . loss Gave tongue when the scent was lost.

Thou art a fool These are hard words for a master of hounds. This lord is nothing if not contemptuous, for he has harder words for the sleeping Sly. He turns easily from blood-sports to peasant-baiting on an elaborate scale.

This were a bed . . . soundly i.e. if sober, he would be cold in such a bed, out-of-doors.

practise Play a trick on.

banquet Dessert, i.e. sweetmeats, fruit and wine, served after the main meal and sometimes in a different room, especially one with a view.

brave Well-dressed.

cannot choose Ellipsis of 'but do so'.

worthless Having no substance.

wanton Alluring.

ewer Basin.

diaper Towel.

disease Illness.

says he is i.e. still 'lunatic'.

kindly Naturally, i.e. without exaggeration. Cf. 1.13.

husbanded with modesty Managed without excess.

As In such a way that.

our true diligence Our care to get every detail correct.

office Household function.

Belike Maybe.

An't Abbreviation of 'and it', if it.

accept our duty Accept our entertainment in return for hospitality.
Soto A farmer's son in *Women Pleased*, by Beaumont and Fletcher.
in happy time At a lucky moment.
cunning Skill (in play-acting).
doubtful of your modesties Afraid you will be unable to exercise self-restraint.
over-eyeing of Noticing.
merry passion Uncontrollable burst of laughter.
veriest antic Most absurdly behaved person.
buttery The 'butlery' (from French *boutellerie*), the room in which liquid refreshment was kept, the 'pantry' being used for solids.
in all suits In every respect (pun on clothes).
Tell him from me . . . action Give him my personal instructions to behave – if he wishes to gain my affection – with airs of distinction.
accomplished Performed.
your humble wife Is this part of the Induction a deliberate contrast with the 'forwardness' of the Shrew?
esteemed him Thought himself.
commanded tears Tears produced for the occasion.
shift Purpose.
in despite Against nature.
Anon Shortly.
usurp the grace Assume the elegance. This 'boy' would be acted by a professional boy-player of women's parts in the Elizabethan theatre; to make his performance in this case look natural, he is represented as gifted in the imitation of women's ways. In asking his page to undertake this offensive task, the lord shows typical disregard of others' feelings.
And how And see how.
haply Perhaps.
abate . . . spleen Check the impulse to loud laughter.

Induction Scene 2

Sly is escorted, having recovered consciousness, into the 'bedroom' in the lord's house, i.e. the gallery above the stage. Here, in downright rustic terms, he rebuts the idea that he is anything but Christopher Sly, a ragged tinker, whose drinking gets him regularly into debt.

He is then told of his great possessions, his retinue of servants, his horses, hounds and hawks, his magnificent tapestries, and, above all, his wife, still beautiful after years of sorrowing for him. He accepts all this – with a request for small beer. When he wonders whether he has done any talking during his long trance, he is assured that the ale-wife and the cronies whom he has mentioned do not exist.

The page trips in and, after bemoaning their long separation, is embarrassed by Sly's prompt suggestion that they go to bed. The boy makes a lame excuse about the doctor's warning that it might bring on the illness again, but is further saved by the entrance of the Players' messenger, who offers their comedy as one way of following the same doctor's advice: that the melancholy that has been the cause of his malady should be dispersed by the kind of mirth their performance will arouse.

Sly agrees and, together with his 'wife', prepares to while away an hour. The stage is thus set for the comedy proper.

Commentary

In this framework to a comedy relying for some of its effect on sophisticated word-play the chief (and almost sole) spectator at first insists on calling a spade a spade. Waking from his drunken bout he prefers ale to wine, rejects the fine 'raiment' it is proposed he should wear (this from the folds of a splendid dressing-gown!) and clings to his humble status as a travelling tinker. It takes a flow of eloquence from the lord and all three servants to convince him that he is (a) really awake and (b) really a lord. The experiment is a success in that Sly comes to accept that any cronies he may have spoken of in his sleep do not exist, and that a whole night's performance has been laid on for his benefit, to banish the strange melancholy that has affected him for many years. A state bedroom of the period would have been large enough, even for the banquet scene in Act V.

The play, as viewed by the audience proper, is to prove one of changing moods, assumed characters, surprise encounters, bizarre tastes in clothes, and contemporary travel on the sort of road from which the tinker himself has just been transported. The 'induction' therefore is like an overture to the main action. Was this Shakespeare's intention? The word 'induction', originally implying the inducing or persuading of someone to believe something contrary to his normal beliefs, is today confined to the installation of such as a priest in his parish. Sly has been duly installed as the 'lord of the manor'.

aloft On the balcony at the back of the stage.
small ale Weak (cheap) ale.
sack A white wine (Spanish *seco*, dry), chiefly imported from Spain and the Canary Isles.
conserves Sweetened fruit.
conserves of beef Salted beef.

overleather Upper part of a shoe.
Heaven cease . . . humour May Heaven put an end to this vain disposition.
Burton-heath There is a Barton-on-the-Heath, about fifteen miles south of Stratford, where one of Shakespeare's uncles lived. Edmund Lambert married Joan Arden, an elder sister of the poet's mother. In a law-suit over a mortgage he seems to have played a sharp trick on his brother-in-law, John Shakespeare (died 1601). Is Sly the son's revenge?
cardmaker 'Cards' were used to comb wool fibres.
transmutation Portentous word for 'change of occupation'.
bear-herd Keeper of a (performing) bear.
Wincot Another village, spelt Wilmcote and pronounced Wincot, four miles north-west of Stratford. It was the birthplace of Mary Arden, Shakespeare's mother, youngest of eight daughters of a substantial yeoman farmer.
on the score Marked up by scoring notches.
sheer ale Strong ale, drunk at 'shearing' time.
bestraught Distracted.
ancient thoughts Former ideas (the reality as compared with dreams).
Apollo God of music. Here the musicians are referred to.
Semiramis Mythical Assyrian queen and oriental goddess of love.
bestrew Strew (with rushes).
trapp'd Decorated with 'trappings', ornaments added to harness.
welkin answer Sky echo.
fetch shrill echoes from the hollow earth i.e. the echoes of their baying will make the earth seem hollow, to produce so much sound.
breathed stags Stags with plenty of wind.
Adonis In Greek legend a handsome young man who preferred his pursuit of hunting to the love offered by Venus (or Cytherea).
wanton with her breath Wave to and fro as she breathes close to them in her hiding-place.
Io Priestess loved by Jupiter (often disguised as a bull) who changed her into a heifer.
as lively painted . . . done Painted in a manner as lifelike as if it were real.
Daphne A nymph pursued by Apollo. She appealed to the gods to save her from his attentions and they changed her into a laurel.
one shall swear she bleeds The viewer will declare he is looking at real blood trickling.
So workmanly With such craftsmanship.
nothing but a lord No less than a lord.
yet Even now.
soft things Cushions (instead of hard boards).
smallest ale Having accepted the idea of his being a lord, Sly cannot so suddenly change his drinking habits.
wit Understanding.
so wak'd as if you slept i.e. behaved as if you were still dreaming. The details follow.

by my fay In faith.
of During.
the hostess of the house The ale-wife.
present her at the leet Have her prosecuted at the manorial court.
stone jug i.e. of uncertain capacity.
reckon'd up Listed by name.
of Greece 'O' th' Green' was suggested by Hammer.
my good amends My restoration to sanity.
thou shalt not lose by it Promising a reward and addressed to one of the serving-men.
Marry Exclamation from 'St Mary'.
fare Sly takes the 'fare' of the page's greeting as meaning 'live well'; the 'cheer' (drink in this case) is plentiful.
noble lord Formal address to a husband on a state occasion.
I know it well Living up to what must still seem a pretence (that he has a wife) or possibly making it clear that he is familiar with the rightful station of a wife.
abandon'd Banished.
expressly charg'd Given strict orders.
stands Holds good.
tarry in despite of Delay against the demands of.
hearing your amendment Learning of your recovery.
melancholy One of the four 'humours', associated with tragedy.
nurse of frenzy Cause of madness.
hear a play A hint of the greater importance of dialogue when stage settings were scanty, if not non-existent.
bars Prevents.
comonty Ignorant mispronunciation of 'comedy'.
household stuff To Sly the very general word 'stuff' means any sort of materials but literary 'matter'.
We shall ne'er be younger A tavern truism, 'Let's enjoy ourselves while we can.'

Revision questions on Induction

1 Summarize the preparations ordered by the lord for the deception of Sly.

2 What would be lost if these two scenes were dispensed with by a producer?

3 What impression does the lord make on you?

Act I Scene 1

Lucentio, son of the wealthy Vincentio, of Pisa, and educated in Florence, has arrived in the great university city of Padua to study philosophy. His lively manservant, Tranio, advises him to mix his serious reading with music and poetry, preferably love-poetry, and largely to follow his own inclination.

In effect, this last recommendation, the now familiar adage, 'Study what you most affect', is almost immediately put into practice. Lucentio has hardly had time to wonder what has happened to his other (and less responsible) servant, Biondello, needed to help in preparing their lodging, when a group of expostulating citizens of Padua come down the street. Baptista, a man of wealth, accompanied by his two daughters, pauses to repeat his decision to the two suitors, Hortensio and the elderly Gremio, for the hand of the younger one, Bianca, not to allow them to woo her before the elder one, Katherina, is married. The temper of Kate and the reluctance of both the men to have anything to do with her are at once apparent. Baptista is firm in his intention to keep Bianca withdrawn and to hire tutors to help her pass the time. He takes Bianca away, followed by a contemptuous Kate, leaving Hortensio and Gremio to forget their rivalry temporarily in order to cooperate in finding the older sister a husband.

As soon as they have departed, Lucentio declares to Tranio his sudden passion for Bianca, whom he has been watching during the argument, while paying little attention to the others. Both simultaneously think of a device to enable him to approach her. The clue has just been given them: their idea is to adopt the disguise of a tutor (in the classics). Lucentio thereupon exchanges some of his garments with Tranio, who is to take his place as the rich Vincentio's son. His other servant, the dilatory Biondello, arrives and gapes at the transformation. He is made to understand that Tranio is to be regarded in public as his master and is told to watch his tongue.

The intrigues of this scene have further fuddled the tinker. When questioned, he professes to be pleased with the play, but wishes it would soon come to an end.

Commentary

By lingering behind at the wharf Biondello is directly responsible for the action of the play: no doubt his powers of observation, later evinced in his detailed description of Petruchio as bridegroom and his spotting of the old Pedant as a substitute father, were being exercised on the shipping in port. It is while waiting for him that Lucentio's attention is drawn to a typical group of gesticulating Paduans. So loud is the discussion that Tranio facetiously suggests that this is some kind of street performance to entertain visitors to the city! It is Tranio, when Lucentio's observation is concentrated on one pretty face, who sees the need for a substitute for Vincentio's son, whose personal presence in Padua is 'expected', a part he is as ready to assume as the lord's page in the preceding scene is in acting a woman's part. The old man himself is to be falsely reported as 'look'd for' in IV,2,117, while his real appearance is totally unexpected.

The indulgent father (Baptista), the two suitors differentiated by age, the love-smitten young traveller and his 'man' (who indeed 'manages' him), the self-contained younger sister, the bogus and the real Vincentio, these are grouped in the sub-plot; the main plot, a straightforward duel between two boisterous temperaments, begins its parallel course in the next scene.

nursery of arts Referring to the famous university, founded 1228.
haply With good luck.
ingenious Intellectual.
first i.e. before me.
traffic Commerce.
Vincentio's son Emendation of Folio 'Vincentio'.
brought up in Florence i.e. educated at the university there.
It shall become . . . conceiv'd It will be to his credit if he strives to realize the ambitions formed for him.
To deck his fortune . . . deeds To make his career a distinguished one because of his virtuous behaviour.
for the time I study During my period of studying.
apply Study, concentrate on. Replaced today by 'ply' as in 'ply a needle'.
that treats . . . achiev'd That (division of philosophy) which defines the kind of happiness obtained by virtuous deeds.
plash Pool. The historic city of Pisa, in decline after its failure to compete with Florence, would be much smaller than the Lombard city of Padua, with its flourishing university.
satiety More than enough.
Mi perdonato Pardon me (Ital.).
affected Inclined.
stoics The Stoici (from *stoa*, the porch where the founder gave his lectures) were a Greek school of philosophers, best remembered today for their calm endurance of suffering.
stocks i.e. lifeless blocks of wood. A pun on 'stoics'.
devote Dedicated.
checks Restraints (on love). Part of a system of balances preserving moderation, in the *Ethics* of the great Greek philosopher, Aristotle.
As Ovid be With the result that Ovid (Latin poet of love, 43 BC–AD 17) is.

abjur'd i.e. the reading of him is rejected.
Balk logic Bandy arguments, indulge in 'chop-logic'.
rhetoric The art of argument.
quicken you Enliven yourself.
your stomach serves you Your inclination directs.
If, Biondello . . . ashore Lucentio's wandering servant puts in an appearance later on.
put us in readiness Prepare ourselves.
as time in Padua shall beget As we shall make during our stay in Padua.
some show The speech and gestures of the new arrivals suggest to Tranio a play put on for their entertainment. And this in the opening scene of a 'show' put on for Sly up in the gallery! A double effect beloved of Shakespeare.
Gremio, a pantaloon An elderly clown (though Gremio is no fool).
cart Put in a cart (used for shaming prostitutes).
I pray you, sir Addressing her father.
stale Prostitute
mates Fellows (would-be husbands).
Iwis Certainly.
it is not . . . heart Marriage is a long way from my desire.
comb your noddle Strike you on the head. This threat to Hortensio is actually carried out in II,1, with a lute!
paint i.e. with the flow of blood.
toward About to take place.
froward Disobedient.
Peace, Tranio Lucentio wishes to gaze on Bianca undisturbed by chatter.
peat Pet (contemptuous).
put finger . . . why i.e. cry – if she knew what to cry about.
content you . . . discontent i.e. get what satisfaction you can from my banishment to studies.
Minerva Roman goddess of wisdom.
strange Harsh (as if an alien to your own daughter).
mew Cage (from falconry).
make her bear . . . her tongue i.e. make Bianca suffer for Kate's tongue.
Prefer them hither Recommended them to come to me.
cunning Clever.
liberal . . . bringing up Sparing no expense in giving them a good education.
appointed hours i.e. told when and where to be. Cf. Bianca's similar objection, in III,1,19.
belike It seems.
Their love is not so great Emended by some to 'Our love', i.e. of Hortensio and himself. Thus this difficult sentence might mean that the pessimistic Gremio, who doubts that Kate will ever be married off, advises blowing their nails together (against the coldness of their suit)

and expelling their love for Bianca by 'fasting it out' (doing without it).

Our cake's dough on both sides Proverbial for complete failure. Or 'both of us have failed'.

wish Recommend.

brooked parle Allowed us to parley together (arrange a truce).

upon advice On further reflection.

loud alarums Frightening shouts.

I had as lief I would as soon.

high cross Market cross (the site for special occasions).

bar in law Treating Baptista's condition as having the force of law.

so far forth friendly . . . till i.e. our cooperation will last till we are free again to compete for Bianca.

have to't Set to.

Happy man be his dole Let happiness be his lot (since he has gained nothing else).

the ring Once given as a prize for winning a race.

I found the effect of love in idleness I fell in love.

in plainness Frankly.

secret In my confidence.

Anna Sister and confidante of Dido, Queen of Carthage, whose unrequited love for Aeneas, according to Virgil, caused her to commit suicide and have her body burnt on a funeral pyre.

rated from the heart i.e. driven from the heart by scolding.

naught remains but so There is nothing to be done but accept it.

Redime . . . minimo ransom yourself from captivity as cheaply as you can. An example (adapted from a line in Terence) in Lily's Latin Grammar, probably in use at Stratford Grammar School.

this contents I am satisfied.

The rest will comfort i.e. what else you have to say will comfort me.

longly For a long time (Cf. Fr. *longuement*).

pith of all Essence of the whole scene.

daughter of Agenor Europa (whose name was given to the continent) was the daughter of a King of Phoenicia. She was carried off to Crete by Jupiter disguised as a bull.

with his knees he kiss'd A bull's salutation.

to stir him Speaking of his master as one oblivious to what has just been said to him about the 'din'.

shrewd Shrewish. Now used only in the sense of 'cunning'.

Because So that.

art thou not advis'd Did you not notice?

cunning Clever.

for my hand By my hand.

bear your part Pretend to be you.

Basta Enough (Ital.).

full All worked out.

port Way of living.

meaner man of Pisa Cf. the 'shallow plash' of Pisa, 1.23.

'Tis hatch'd The plot is formed.

Uncase Remove your hat and cloak.
colour'd Garments of various colours distinguished the master from the man in a garb of uniform blue.
charm Cast a spell over.
in another sense i.e. not taking his son's place (an act which in V,1 gives the old man a shock).
Whose sudden sight . . . eye The unexpected sight of whom has, by striking my eye, enslaved me.
fellow i.e. fellow-servant.
frame your manners to the time Behave towards each of us as the situation requires.
to save my life In two senses (1) real, to win Bianca, (2) pretended, to escape execution.
countenance Bearing.
descried Detected.
Ne'er a whit Not at all.
Would I were so too i.e. similarly promoted.
So could I Does this mean 'I could wish also that I were Lucentio, in order to win Bianca'? Tranio has begun to play his part with gusto, giving instructions to Biondello in the presence of Lucentio.
mind Pay attention to.
Saint Anne Mother of St Mary. First given her day in the Calendar in 1584.

Act I Scene 2

Another (and more important) visitor arrives in Padua. Unlike Lucentio, Petruchio has friends already in the great city, and he has in fact made his way to the house of the best friend he has here. He is accompanied by his diminutive servant, Grumio, who seizes every opportunity for clowning. This time he overdoes it and his tempestuous master, trying to 'knock' some sense into his head, gives a foretaste of the violence of which he is capable.

Hortensio emerges to greet them and is told that the object of Petruchio's visit is to marry well and spend some of his inheritance seeing the world. Hortensio immediately seizes the opportunity of carrying out the plan agreed with Gremio in the last scene, to produce a husband for Kate. For a friend he is a shade dishonest in recommending to Petruchio a wife rich, but 'plain'. When he is surprised by Petruchio's readiness to marry anyone with money, he makes doubly sure of the bargain by his praise of Kate's beauty and accomplishments, adding that her one fault is her shrewish temper.

Petruchio is eager to set off in search of Kate, and Hortensio accepts an invitation to accompany him, as he is in love with her younger sister, whom, he explains, no one may court until Kate is married.

Hortensio's ardour is such that, though Kate now looks like being swiftly married, he schemes to get near Bianca (and so forestall Gremio) by asking Petruchio to introduce him in the guise of a music tutor. Nothing deters Petruchio, not even this transparent move to exploit him as part of a wooer's intrigue.

At this point Gremio is observed discussing with *his* hired tutor, Lucentio, disguised as a schoolmaster called Cambio, whom he has encountered somewhere in the interval, the books to be read with Bianca. The two groups then greet each other. Gremio introduces his tutor, and, for his part, Hortensio professes to know a gentleman who knows a teacher of music (himself, a fact he does not wish Gremio to know). He presents Petruchio as their common saviour, a suitor for Kate who remains quite undaunted by Gremio's grim warnings.

What seems a needless complication at this stage is the appearance of Tranio (deputizing for Lucentio, himself present in disguise as Cambio), boldly proclaiming his suit to Bianca. Lucentio's reasons for this manoeuvre are made clear in Act IV: to decoy Baptista away when the marriage agreement is being settled; and to enable Tranio to persuade Hortensio to join him in renouncing Bianca. Tranio pretends he has not seen Bianca, but is acting, like Petruchio, on hearsay. The way is now open for the wooing of Bianca, but, until Kate is actually married, the three suitors suspend their rivalry and meanwhile proceed to entertain their rescuer.

By now the doubtless bewildered spectator in the gallery-bedroom, whose own personal identity has been troubling him, is heard snoring away, oblivious of the model 'wife' by his side. The rest of his story is a blank so far as the printed stage directions go.

Commentary

It is Hortensio's friendship with Petruchio that leads to the discovery of a potential husband for Katherina. If the last scene was marked by wordy argument, this one opens with blows that are symbolic of events to come. Grumio's clown-like wit constantly gets him into trouble; his cry for help would indicate that this is a public street, with citizens not far off.

Unlike Lucentio, who is enslaved by beauty, Petruchio is out to both 'wive and thrive', and looks are secondary, he claims, to wealth. He is prepared to wed a rich bride, however ugly she may be. Is this an assumed posture disguising a real appreciation of women, just as his extreme rudeness later masks a growing affection? His confidence, needed in one the others are looking to as a shrew-tamer, is based on the possession of ample funds and an undaunted experience of sea-storms and land-battles.

The accepted suitors to Bianca find their relief at meeting one bold enough to take on Katherina balanced by the arrival on the scene of the third aspirant to Bianca's hand in Tranio, whose contrived intervention later proves superfluous. There is, too, a certain artificiality in Petruchio having to explain the situation to this newcomer when he himself has only just been informed of it. In fact, the dropping of the dialogue from Tranio's entry to the end of the scene, as well as the minor developments that follow, would be no loss to the play. If it is an addition by an inferior hand, it comes curiously between Grumio's reference to a 'good dinner' in l.216 and the meal actually proposed by Tranio and greeted enthusiastically by Grumio and his fellow-page.

Lucentio, a spectator in the last scene, is here himself watched from the wings until Hortensio introduces Petruchio, and then he in turn looks on as Tranio deputizes for him.

Verona Apostrophizing his native city from where he now is.
approved Tested.
knock The extended pun goes from knocking at the door to knocking a person down, through Grumio's persistent misunderstanding of the fashionable *ethic dative* (knock 'for me').
rebused Malapropism for 'abused'.
pate Head.
will it not be? Are you going to knock or not?
ring it i.e. ring at the gate. Punning on 'wringing' Grumio's ear.
solfa Utter some notes (of pain).
My old friend Grumio! Addressing the servant first, possibly because Grumio's struggle catches the eye; then Hortensio sees who is tormenting him. Petruchio's first words of greeting are 'Come you to part the fray?' Hortensio speaks to Grumio as to one lying on the ground.
Con tutto il cuore, ben trovato With all my heart, well-met.
Alla nostra casa ben venuto, molto honorato signor mio To our house welcome, most honoured sir.
compound Settle.
'leges in Latin i.e. alleges in what sounds like Latin to an English stage character in an Italian setting!

being Agrees with 'his master'.
two and thirty, a pip out One more than the winning score in a game of cards (as in cribbage), i.e. beyond himself.
Grumio's pledge i.e. I will bail him out of trouble.
heavy chance Serious set-to.
gale In nautical terms a strong wind, in poetry a gentle breeze, this word must be figurative in referring to what has been a journey overland.
in a few In a few words.
haply Perchance.
come abroad In contemporary use for going from one city to another.
come roundly Speak frankly.
wish Recommend.
ill-favour'd Plain-featured. Hortensio presumably hopes that the discovery of Kate's good looks will close the trap.
not wish Not recommend (because of her looks).
burden Bass accompaniment.
wooing dance i.e. as I dance to music, so I woo to the tune of money.
foul Ugly.
Florentius' love In Gower's *Confessio Amantis* an ugly hag, accepted by Florentius in return for the answer to a riddle, turned into a beautiful girl.
Sibyl An aged prophetess.
Xanthippe Wife of the philosopher Socrates, and a shrew.
moves me not i.e. not from my resolution.
not removes . . . edge in me Does not blunt the keenness of my love.
aglet-baby A doll decorated with 'aglets' (Fr. *aiguillette*), metal-tagged laces; or a doll-shaped 'aglet'.
trot Hag. The word may have suggested horse diseases, of which the number was traditionally fifty.
thus far in i.e. Petruchio is interested in Hortensio's proposition.
state Financial position.
board her Attack her. From the naval word for forcing a way on to an enemy vessel.
crack i.e. with thunder, like the guns used to repel boarders.
give you over Part company. In order to visit Baptista.
humour Mood.
And If (three times in this speech).
rail in his rope-tricks Use strong language in his 'rope-tricks', actions deserving of the gallows. 'Rhetoric' has been suggested, and as this employs figures of speech (the word 'figure' is used in the next sentence), the word 'trope' (figure of speech) may have been corrupted to 'rope'. Editors are nothing if not ingenious.
stand him Stand up to him.
figure There is pun on the rhetorical figure just referred to and the physical sense of 'disfigure' or deform.
cat Pun on Kate(?). Eyes half-closed after a beating?
keep Keeping. Possible allusion to the keep of a castle, followed up by

the use of 'hold', meaning either 'strong-hold' or 'captivity'.

Supposing . . . impossible Suggesting that Baptista, jealous of any husband for his favourite Bianca, thinks his condition (Kate's marriage) cannot be fulfilled.

For Because of.

rehears'd Described.

order Instruction; measure; decision.

grace A favour.

offer Introduce.

Well seen Expert.

Here's no knavery! Ironical.

A proper stripling and an amorous Presumably applied ironically to Gremio.

O, very well Spoken in approval and not impatience.

the note A list of Cambio's reading requirements.

at any hand On any account.

read no other lectures to her Study no other texts with her.

mend it with a largess Increase it (Baptista's fee) with an extra gift of money.

Take your paper The 'note' already referred to.

them i.e. the books.

As for my patron As the man who recommended me as tutor.

O this learning, what a thing it is! An expression of envious admiration, not contempt.

woodcock A bird easily caught and so a symbol of stupidity.

Trow you? Would you believe?

Fit for her turn Suited to her tastes.

help me to another Assist me in finding another. The post has already been filled by himself, but it would not do for Gremio to know.

in duty to fair Bianca i.e. both have now helped her father by supplying tutors.

bags Money-bags.

indifferent Equally.

Upon agreement . . . liking Once we agree to his conditions.

say'st me so? You don't say so! Expressing surprise at Petruchio's seeing no harm in what he has heard of Kate.

What countryman? Where do you come from?

My fortune lives for me A callous contrast with a dead father.

were strange Would be unusually harsh.

or I'll hang her In the unlikely case of Petruchio's not wooing her, or in the proverbial sense: to prevent a bad marriage (with another).

chafed with sweat Irritated by his sweat. In heraldry (of great social importance in Shakespeare's day) *chafant* was the term to describe a boar in a rage.

ordnance Guns.

a chestnut in a farmer's fire A method of finding out lovers' fates. An explosion could indicate a quarrel, or the direction taken by the chestnut point to the future spouse.

fear Frighten.
bugs Bogeys (same word. Cf. Welsh 'bwg', ghost). A bugbear was originally a hobgoblin in the shape of a bear used to frighten children into obedience.
happily Fortunately.
as sure of a good dinner Showing his confidence in his master's success.
brave Dressed in his master's finery.
is't he you mean? Biondello, a stranger to the city, speaks as if he were familiar with the neighbourhood, and acts as if he and Tranio ('Lucentio') had only just met.
you mean not her to He is about to use a word like 'approach'.
him and her i.e. Baptista and the one daughter his mind is set on.
Not her that chides Petruchio warns 'Lucentio' off Kate, even before he has seen her.
the maid you talk of Bianca, 'chiders' having been eliminated.
To whom my father is not all unknown Tranio is guessing; this claim is shown to be false when, in V,1, Baptista fails to recognize Vincentio.
Leda's daughter Helen, wife of Menelaus, who was carried off to Troy by Paris (1.245) and was thus the cause of the Trojan War.
to speed alone To be the only one to succeed.
out-talk us i.e. with his classical allusions (one of Tranio's accomplishments 'approved' in I,1).
give him head . . . jade Allow him to gallop freely and, like an inferior steed, he will quickly flag.
to what end are all these words? Petruchio is a man of action and short speeches. Impatient with displays of learning, he is doubtless also somewhat puzzled by the number of suitors springing up to court Bianca.
Hercules Also called Alcides after his grandfather, Alcaeus, his strength was legendary. Twelve superhuman tasks were imposed on him, known as 'The Labours of Hercules'.
hearken for Are lying in wait for.
stead us Come to our rescue.
break the ice . . . feat Two ways of expressing the hardness of the task of wooing Kate.
Achieve Win.
whose hap He whose fortune.
ingrate Ungrateful (over the expenses referred to above).
conceive Express the matter.
gratify Satisfy with payment.
rest . . . beholding Remain indebted.
contrive Plan to spend.
quaff carouses Drink toasts.
adversaries Opposed counsel in law cases.
strive i.e. in court.
O excellent motion The servants anticipate a drinking session.
your ben venuto (lit.) Welcome i.e. the one to wish you welcome, in other words, be your host.

Revision questions on Act I

1 Describe the mood and the circumstances in which (a) Katherina and (b) Petruchio appear in these scenes. What are your first impressions?

2 In how many ways are characters in this Act indebted for services rendered by others?

3 Contrast Tranio and Grumio as attendants on their masters. Are the differences in any way connected with the characters of Lucentio and Petruchio?

Act II Scene 1

Kate, having tied Bianca's hands, taunts her about her suitors; even the arrival of her father fails to change her hostility towards her demure sister. It seems that she resents (1) Bianca's refusal to say which suitor she likes best, and (2) her father's preference for Bianca, made evident by his having previously allowed suitors to approach the younger sister before her own marriage. Although, as announced by Baptista in I,1, the customary condition has now been made (at Kate's prompting?), Kate still fumes over her apparent destiny as an elder, unmarried sister, after the reluctance shown by Hortensio and Gremio in that scene. She leaves the stage to plan revenge.

There now arrive, as planned in I,2, suitors to both daughters. First Petruchio asks Baptista's permission to court Kate (whom he has not yet seen), and in payment for his reception in the house offers his friend Hortensio as the music tutor 'Licio'. Gremio (not recognizing Hortensio in his humbler garb) now pushes forward *his* contribution to the tutoring of Bianca in the form of Lucentio, whom he knows only as 'Cambio', a language-teacher. There is dramatic irony in Gremio's hope to advance his own case with Bianca in thus bringing into close touch with her her latest and most passionate admirer.

Baptista has now obtained what he asked for: a potential husband for Kate, and tutors for Bianca. His attention is next drawn to Tranio, apparently a stranger to the city, and he finds himself confronted by a third suitor for his favourite daughter. The newcomer's share in her education is a gift of books, on which the name of the real owner, Lucentio, must have been written, for Baptista addresses him (Tranio) by his assumed name without having been told it. Both Baptista and Gremio seem to have failed to recognize Hortensio in 'Licio'. If Lucentio has recognized him, he gives no sign of it in this or the next scene.

A servant conducts the two tutors to their pupils. Petruchio agrees with Baptista on Kate's dowry from her father, and his own provision in case of her widowhood. He is declaring his ardour and unshakeable determination in his suit when Hortensio returns with a damaged head – Kate has attacked him with her lute, to the accompaniment of some violent language. This mishap makes Petruchio more enamoured than ever and he is eager to see her. Baptista takes Hortensio out to take a turn with the milder Bianca (with whom, one may well understand, Lucentio has started to make some progress) and offers to send Kate to meet her unexpected suitor.

Petruchio, like some general soliloquizing before a fateful battle, prepares for the encounter by rehearsing his method: to praise her for the opposite of every mood she manifests and to act contrary to everything she says or does. The hero and heroine have the stage to themselves, in contrast to the fluctuating groups that precede and follow this duologue. There is first the long and (in the reading) tedious play and counter-play on words (punishing each other with puns!); then the extempore purple passage with its flashes of poetry; finally the overbearing peroration, in which, armed with her father's consent down to the last details of her dowry, he declares his sense of destiny to convert her from her wild state to something more conventional.

When Baptista reappears he is reproached by his termagant daughter for contracting her off to such an outrageous husband. Petruchio retorts with a false, but somehow convincing, explanation (and one which is probably not without effect upon the one he is wooing in this whirlwind fashion) that Kate's temper has been assumed by her to conceal her real nature; further (a subtle stroke worthy of some modern brainwasher) she is, by secret agreement between them, to continue her outward shrewishness! He goes on to depict an entirely fictitious Kate, who has clung passionately to him, and, in fact, won his love outright. Having thus cut the ground from under her feet, he announces his departure for Venice to buy suitable clothes. Baptista blesses the pair, who leave, affianced husband dragging his wife by the hand.

This grim battle of wills is succeeded by a much more unseemly auction (at her father's instigation) for the hand of Bianca, now that Kate has been accounted for. The competition is between Gremio and Tranio before the father, while the two real suitors are, as represented in the following scene, rivals in the presence of the daughter. Gremio, for all his wealth, is outmatched by Tranio, who presumably should know the extent of the possessions of his master, Lucentio's rich father, Vincentio, but who may well exaggerate to keep Gremio out of the running, or for the sheer fun of it. When, however, Baptista requires a guarantee of the winning offer from 'Lucentio's' father, who may, as Gremio points out, be predeceased by his son and not keep his son's promise, Tranio – living up to his reputation for resourcefulness – in order to spare his young master any disturbance of his courtship, determines to find someone in Padua to act as Vincentio.

Commentary

There is some confusion of tutors and pupils in this scene, in which the two plots are closely interwoven, though this may well pass unnoticed during the performance. The stage direction at l.39 is precise in announcing three groups, all fresh from banqueting together: old Gremio, accompanied by his newly engaged tutor, Lucentio, in disguise as Cambio, teacher of languages and destined for the tuition of Bianca; Petruchio, introducing Hortensio as Licio, teacher of music and mathematics, apparelled as a musician and offered as tutor to the termagant sister (is this 'entrance' to his wooing of Katherina a typical trick on his part?); and thirdly the intrusive Tranio, playing to the full the part of his master, and bringing no tutor, but the means – books and instrument – for the other two, to support his surprise suit.

Neither of Baptista's daughters might be expected to be in a mood for academic instruction, but the old man keeps to his plan, despatching a servant to take the 'impostor' tutors to their respective charges (an errand presumably below his personal dignity). After Hortensio's misadventure with Katherina he is sent back to take turns with 'Cambio', as seen in the next Act.

To Petruchio lovemaking is just another combat, and Katherina's violence is a challenge. No sooner has he boasted that he is ready like an immovable mountain to endure an irresistible storm than the battered Hortensio appears.

to my elders i.e. to you as my elder sister.
dissemble Tell an untruth.

Minion Spoilt darling (Fr. *mignon*).
belike Probably.
fair Handsomely dressed.
you jest i.e. in envying me the suit paid by an old man.
then all the rest was so i.e. this was meant as seriously as the rest.
dame Like 'mistress', an honourable word used in contempt.
hilding Contemptible creature.
suffer me Allow me (to go after her).
she must have a husband i.e. you will indulge her desire to get married, although you know the offer of my hand will not be taken up by anyone; I shall end up as the unmarried elder sister at her marriage. Dramatic irony; the audience waits in expectation of the arrival of Petruchio, which is not long delayed.
dance barefoot Traditional performance by spinster sisters older than the bride.
lead apes in hell Belief in this destiny for old maids was widespread but of unknown origin.
a mean man i.e one of humble appearance. Taken probably from Lucentio's own description, 'meaner man of Pisa' (I,1,205).
orderly Gradually.
forward Bold.
for an entrance to my entertainment As payment for my reception (in Baptista's house).
not for your turn Unsuited to you.
Saving your tale With no disrespect for your account of yourself.
Baccare A piece of dog-Latin become proverbial, 'get back'.
I would fain be doing I am eager to get courting.
Neighbour Addressing Baptista.
grateful Either, deserving of gratitude, or as an expression of gratitude.
myself I myself.
Rheims A university founded there c.1550 rapidly acquired a reputation.
preferment of Maintaining the prior claim (to marriage) of.
favour Favourable reception.
a simple instrument A lute, given by Baptista to Hortensio, as are the books to Cambio. They were brought in by Tranio.
their worth is great i.e. by the mere act of accepting them, you give them value.
mighty man A man in a position of power.
orchard Garden.
passing Very.
so i.e. welcome.
in possession i.e. to have immediately on marriage.
widowhood Settlement on her when she becomes a widow.
specialties Specific contracts.
special thing To Baptista, Kate's love is special only in being difficult to obtain.

peremptory Given to commanding.
happy be thy speed May you be so fortunate as to succeed.
to the proof Metal-tested.
That shakes not i.e. the winds do not shake the mountains.
broke Gashed.
fume From 'fume and fret'. Another pun.
amazed Stunned.
As on a pillory As if I had my head in a pillory.
twangling Jack A fellow making discordant noises.
As had she As if she had.
Proceed in practice Continue your instruction.
attend Wait for.
rail Scold.
hard Pun on heard (probably pronounced 'hard'). She means, 'You must be partially deaf and not caught my full name.'
bonny Handsome.
of Kate Hall i.e. a lady of good family.
dainties are all Kates All dainties are 'cates' (delicacies, used in the plural).
Take this of me Accept what I have to say.
Kate of my consolation Kate, my consoler.
sounded Celebrated.
not so deeply i.e. not so highly (praised). Playing on another meaning of 'sound', to test the depth of.
in good time i.e. you are quickly 'moved', having only just met me.
movable A piece of furniture that is not a fixture.
joint-stool Stool made by joining pieces together, i.e. nothing much to look at.
hit it i.e. described me exactly.
bear Carry burdens.
No such jade i.e. I am no worthless horse. Not, as now, limited to females.
swain Rustic.
yet as heavy i.e. at my normal weight I am still too light for you to seize.
buzz Pun on 'be' (bee).
buzzard Hawk that cannot be trained, therefore stupid. A return pun.
turtle Dove. The easy prey of a stupid buzzard.
for a turtle i.e. (mis)taking me for a dove.
as he takes a buzzard As the dove catches a buzzing insect.
lose your arms i.e. be deprived of your coat-of-arms for ceasing to be a gentleman by striking me with your bodily arms.
books i.e. records of coats of arms (popular in Tudor times).
What is your crest? A question put to one seeking to have his arms recorded, but Kate is using the 'crest' to arrive at a 'coxcomb', a conceited person, from the cock's comb of the jester.
combless Without a comb or anything to boast about.
craven i.e. a cock which refused to fight, from a craven knight who 'craved' his life in defeat.

a crab Wild apple, sour to taste.
glass Mirror.
wither'd i.e. old (like an over-ripe crab apple).
I care not I love not.
chafe Ruffle. Opposite of 'passing gentle' in next line.
coy Stand-offish.
look askance Cast a questioning look.
conference Conversation.
halt Limp.
whom thou keep'st command Give orders to your own household.
Dian Diana, goddess of hunting and, in some cults, of chastity. Worshipped in groves.
extempore Impromptu.
witty Intellectual.
keep you warm From proverbial 'enough wit to keep oneself warm'.
so I mean So I intend.
nill you Won't you. Cf. 'willy-nilly'.
for your turn To suit you.
by this light i.e. swearing by it.
wild Kate Punning on the 'wildcat' suggested by Gremio in I,2,194.
Conformable Conforming to instructions.
how speed you? How are you succeeding?
dumps Low spirits.
promise Declare (with no reference to the future).
Jack Low fellow.
face the matter out Brazen it out.
amiss Falsely.
policy Tactics.
hot Hot-tempered.
Grissel Griselda, the patient wife in *The Clerk's Tale*, by Chaucer.
Lucrece She took her life after Tarquin, tyrant king of Rome, had raped her.
speeding Success.
good night our part Goodbye to our chances of wooing Bianca.
for myself i.e. not to carry out your plan.
She vied so fast She placed higher and higher bids. From a card game.
twink Flash.
'Tis a world to see It's marvellous to note. 'World' was used loosely for 'something to wonder at'.
alone i.e. one man and one woman together. This glimpse of marital control is as false as his portrait of Kate!
meacock Effeminate.
shrew The first time Petruchio has used the title word for Kate.
o'Sunday From a ballad, 'For I'm to be married o'Sunday'. With six Tudor working days, Sunday was the most suitable day for a wedding.
play a merchant's part Take a commercial risk.
mart Bargain.

a commodity lay fretting Goods which were deteriorating in store (Kate being at home unmarried).
gain i.e. quiet at home.
perish on the seas i.e. Petruchio will be the death of her.
quiet in the match Is this Baptista's fatherly feeling looking for a happy outcome for his daughter, or merely the thought of relief?
a quiet catch Ironic reference to Kate.
Skipper Youngster.
compound Settle.
he of both The one of you two.
assure Guarantee.
lave Wash.
Tyrian Purple. From a dye made at Tyre.
arras counterpoints Counterpanes made in Arras, France.
tents Testers over the beds.
Valance . . . needlework Drapery (from Valence-on-the-Rhone) hanging from a canopy and embroidered in gold thread in Venetian style.
milch-kine to the pail Cows milked into pails for human consumption.
answerable to this portion In proportion to this dowry.
struck in years Overtaken by old age. Mod. 'stricken'.
rich Pisa walls The 'shallow plash' of I,1 had wealth out of proportion to its size.
ducats Coins first issued by the Duke of Apulia (hence the name). The common European currency and familiar to audiences of *The Merchant of Venice.*
by the year of Annual rent from.
jointure Settlement.
argosy Large merchant ship.
Marseilles road The 'road' is the roadstead or harbour.
galliasses Large galleys.
tight Water-tight, therefore in good condition.
twice as much i.e. as I have already offered.
If you like me Spoken to Baptista.
from all the world Alone above all competitors.
firm promise i.e. of Bianca for the 'greatest dower' (l.336).
assurance Guarantee.
a cavil A quibble.
set foot under thy table i.e. live at your expense and so be dependent on you.
a toy i.e. What a joke!.
An old Italian fox Himself or the father of 'Lucentio'?
A vengeance Tranio is angry at the suggestion of Gremio that his 'father' should guarantee the settlement.
fac'd it with a card of ten Bluffed his opponent who may hold higher cards.
to do my master good i.e. by not disturbing his courtship of Bianca.
suppos'd Lucentio must get a father i.e. he, Tranio (since as 'Lucentio'

he has no real father) must reverse the course of nature and 'beget' a father.

Revision questions on Act II

1 Wealth was proverbial in the 16th-century cities of Northern Italy and highly respected in expanding Tudor England. What various attitudes to money and property can you find in this Act?

2 In this first encounter with Katherina, Petruchio relies solely on his verbal skills. By what stages does he reach the triumphant announcement of their forthcoming marriage?

3 Gremio is present throughout most of this scene. What surprises does he meet with, and what would surprise him if he knew?

Act III Scene 1

While 'Lucentio' and Gremio have been outbidding each other for Bianca's hand, the contest between the real suitors, both disguised as tutors, has been going on in another part of Baptista's house. This short scene exhibits them revealing in turn to Bianca their identity and devotion. Lucentio has a copy of Ovid's *Art of Love*, Hortensio a lute.

Hortensio claims, by virtue of the superiority of his art, the right to give Bianca a music lesson, under the assumed name of 'Licio', before the reading of Ovid by Lucentio, under his assumed name of 'Cambio'. The latter retorts that the chief function of music is as relaxation after hard intellectual effort. Bianca settles the matter by telling 'Licio' to tune his lute, presumably a fresh one after his treatment by Katherina. The translating of Ovid phrase by phrase has passed into a lovers' dialogue, which the musician cannot overhear, through the sound of his tuning. This is followed, at Bianca's request, by the music lesson, which takes the form of a device rivalling 'Cambio's': the notes of the scale are annotated by 'Licio's' piecemeal declaration of love.

Bianca is expressing her preference for more traditional music when a messenger summons her to help prepare for her sister's wedding. Hortensio, his suspicions aroused, basely declares his readiness to find a substitute for Bianca if she should love another.

Commentary

'Where left we last?' is a subtle indication that during Petruchio's tempestuous wooing of her sister, Bianca has been left alone with Lucentio, yet their stage conversation here reveals only slight progress! In fact, the demure younger sister deliberately misconstrues the Latin phrases, though dropping a hint that 'Cambio' should not give up hope. She switches abruptly to Hortensio and, when sent for by her father, swiftly escapes from having to be pleasant with two wooers taking their turns. She resents being competed for in a matter in which the choice should be hers and, like Katherina, objects to being 'tied to hours'.

There is a curious parallel between the genuine if unnecessary secrecy of this courtship and Petruchio's publicly proclaimed but fictitious bargain with Katherina, by which she is pretending to be keeping her real affection concealed under outbursts of temper.

Fiddler Spoken contemptuously. Many fiddlers were beggars, and 'Licio' is a lute-player.

forbear From pressing his attentions.

wrangling pedant Argumentative schoolmaster (teacher of languages).

this is the patroness Line 4 has three missing syllables. Marshall makes the sensible suggestion: 'this, her sister, is'.

lecture Reading of texts.

his usual pain His daily labour.

read philosophy In the university sense. However, as instructed by Gremio, this tutor has brought poetry by Ovid, a poet of love.

serve in your harmony Bring in your music (much as the next course in a meal).

bear these braves Put up with these outrageous remarks.

breeching scholar A schoolboy in need of breeches or a whipping.

the whiles Meanwhile. Advice to prevent him from overhearing the conversational type of construing which she and Lucentio have adopted.

ere you have tun'd Meaning either that he is a poor musician or that Lucentio is going to be restricted. In this dialogue Bianca shows some of her sister's spirit.

Where left we last? Where did we leave off? The reading may be presumed to have begun while Hortensio was attempting to instruct Kate and been interrupted by his return with Baptista.

Hic ibat . . . senis Here flowed the (River) Simois, here is the Sigeian land, here once had stood the royal palace of old Priam (King of Troy). The Folio has the first *hic*, 'here', instead of *hac*, 'by this way', as in the Latin text of Ovid's *Heroides*.

Construe i.e. translate phrase by phrase alternately text and English rendering.
bearing my port Behaving as if he were I.
beguile the old pantaloon Deceive Gremio (whom Lucentio seems to fear most and who, unknown to Lucentio, has just been outbid by his imaginative proxy).
the base knave that jars The low fellow who is spoiling the conversation. The musical 'bass' was spelt thus until the last century.
Pedascule Coined by Hortensio from 'pedant' and diminutive suffix '-culus' (cf. *homunculus*) to mean 'little schoolmaster'. He forgets that he himself is disguised as a tutor.
I may believe i.e. in your love.
for sure Aeacides . . . grandfather This reference to the next line in Ovid is a cover-up answer to her mistrust (Hortensio is listening).
I must believe my master A delightful piece of ambiguity.
upon that doubt Either about the meaning of Aeacides or about Lucentio's profession of love.
pleasant Teasing.
in three parts A sarcastic reference to three voices trying to make harmony.
formal Insistent on formality or correct arrangement.
withal Besides.
but I am deceived Unless I am mistaken.
rudiments of art Elementary rules.
gamut The scale of notes (six in Tudor times). They are listed below.
fairly drawn Neatly executed.
past my gamut Beyond the elementary (ABC) stage in music.
read the gamut of Hortensio Handing her the paper on which he has written his love message spaced out over the notes in a similar fashion to Lucentio's translation of Ovid. Another coincidental 'invention'! Hortensio thus abandons his disguise both by voice and on paper. Is this a surprise to Bianca, to whom he has for some time been an acknowledged suitor? If not, she maintains the deception of both in the presence of both.
Gamut Originally, as here, the lowest note (based on Greek *gamma*).
accord Concord, harmony.
clef Musical key.
Old fashions i.e. musical techniques, not professions of love.
so nice to So fastidious as to want to.
odd inventions Curious new ideas.
tomorrow is the wedding-day Petruchio has little time for purchases. The swiftness of the courting is matched by the swiftness of events.
stale A decoy-pigeon, used in hawking; hence any person acting as a lure.
Seize thee that list Let him take you that cares.
ranging Straying.
be quit with thee by changing Get even with you by giving my love to another.

Act III Scene 2

The wedding-party is assembled, but the bridegroom is late. The bride, put to shame by this marriage (forced upon her) with a rude practical joker, dissolves into tears (a symptom of change?) and goes back into the house, attended by her sister. Biondello rushes in to announce the imminent approach of the bridegroom in old clothes, on a worn-out horse and attended by a grotesquely garbed servant. The unabashed Petruchio strides onto the scene, calling out for his bride. Brushing aside protests, and promising explanations later, he seeks Kate within the house, preparatory to their attendance at church.

Tranio takes this opportunity to explain to Lucentio his plan, as the 'successful suitor' to Bianca, to get someone to represent Lucentio's father, whose presence will be needed for the signing of the guarantee of 'Lucentio's' settlement to be made on Bianca. Lucentio himself would prefer an elopement, if it were not for the watchfulness of Hortensio. Tranio stresses the advantage of awaiting an opportunity to outwit the others.

The shortness of this interval indicates the brevity of the disorderly ceremony in which Kate is wedded to Petruchio. Gremio escapes to describe it. His account of the bad language, the knocking down of the priest, the throwing of the wine in the sexton's face and, as a climax, the violent embrace of the bride by the groom, is as fantastic as the earlier account of Petruchio's shocking appearance. To cap all this, the wedding party, now back on the stage, are told by Petruchio that he and his newly wedded wife must make an immediate departure on mysterious but important business.

Kate's last defiance, by refusing to accompany him, is borne down by her husband's loud proclamation that he now owns her, followed by a challenge to anyone to obstruct them. If no other line in this play were by Shakespeare, the following lines, whose delicious irony redeems the farcical excesses in this long scene, cannot be denied his stamp:

Fear not, sweet wench, they shall not touch thee, Kate:
I'll buckler thee against a million.

This comes from the pen that drew Benedick's duel with Beatrice in *Much Ado About Nothing* and King Harry's wooing of *his* Catherine.

Old Gremio still thinks that it is Petruchio who is in trouble, while Baptista invites 'Lucentio' and Bianca to occupy the places left vacant by bridegroom and bride. The real Lucentio is content to watch from a less prominent position his 'well approved' Tranio 'bearing his port' and sitting beside his Bianca.

Commentary

A notable absentee from this wedding is Hortensio, whose courtship of Bianca, like that of Gremio, his sparring partner, would now seem to have been facilitated by the marriage of the elder sister; however, he has just expressed his doubts about the lady he has been known publicly to be courting, and in the next act only too readily abandons further interest in her, as well as eagerly discarding his disguise as a humble tutor – he is rather ashamed of what was his own suggestion!

One purpose in Tranio's disguise as Lucentio, and hinted vaguely at in I,1,245–7, was as a third wooer to discourage Hortensio (the younger of the two official rivals) from going on with his suit. When this purpose is achieved in Act IV Scene 2 and duly reported by Tranio to the couple now openly in love, there seems to be no further need for master and man to play each other's parts. Nevertheless Tranio takes upon himself the task of imposing a substitute father on Baptista to guarantee the extravagant offers he has made on behalf of Lucentio, which trick creates further comedy to lengthen the plot.

The farcical nature of this ceremony, designed to humiliate Katherina utterly, is brought home to the audience's imagination by two detailed and fantastic accounts of (1) Petruchio's appearance and (2) his behaviour in church. Indeed, as in the reception at Petruchio's home, his worst antics are not shown on stage but vividly reported.

In this scene the two plots are ingeniously interwoven. Tranio, besides his concern about the dowry he has promised, is anxious that the marriage of Katherina shall not fall through and so thwart that of Bianca; he does his best to persuade Petruchio to change his mean outfit for more seemly clothes. His master leaves him full scope to make decisions, content to concentrate on winning Bianca, if necessary by a secret marriage. Having observed Petruchio's way of taking possession, Lucentio mutters 'I'll keep mine own, despite of all the world'. Meanwhile old Baptista, his elaborate wedding feast rudely deprived of original bride and groom, is content, perhaps relieved, to install Bianca and the man he knows as Lucentio in the places of honour. For several scenes the real Lucentio flits in and out of the wings, with or without Bianca; here we must imagine him taking his seat, as if a guest at a banquet honouring his bride-to-be at the top table, who is sitting beside his own servant playing the part of an accepted suitor, but actually about to organize his master's run-away marriage – an unusual situation in real life!

No shame but mine I am the only one to be ashamed. Perhaps it is a disappointed Kate who speaks.
rudesby Rude fellow.
spleen Capricious impulses.
Who woo'd in haste . . . leisure An adaptation of the proverbial 'wed in haste and repent at leisure'.
Hiding . . . behaviour Masking his cruelty with his rudeness.
to be noted for In order to acquire a reputation as.
means but well Tranio acts a very sincere concern for his 'courtship' of Bianca, dependent as it is on Kate's getting married. His character sketch of Petruchio is based on very recent acquaintance.
stays him from his word Delays him from keeping his promise.
merry Given to joking.
old news The play on 'news' is a first hint of the worn-out apparel in which Petruchio is coming to his wedding.
Why no, sir Meaning he has not yet come *here*, but is on the way. There is a similar quibble in l.77 on his *horse* coming.
jerkin Close-fitting jacket, often of leather.
turned i.e. inside out.
candle cases Candles could be stored in old boots.
town armoury i.e. municipal equipment subject to neglect.
chapeless Without a 'chape', metal tip to the scabbard.
with two broken points These cannot be the laces tying breeches to jerkin, but possibly part of the sword furnishings.
hipped With a bad hip. The majority of the clinical terms that follow are not to be found anywhere else in Shakespeare.
of no kindred Not of the same pair.
glanders Swellings beneath a horse's jaws with discharges from the nostrils.
like to mose in the chine 'Mose' is a misprint difficult to emend. The 'chine' was the backbone.
lampass A swelling of the mouth.
fashions i.e. farcy, or tumours.
windgalls Swellings on the legs above the fetlocks.
sped with spavins Done for, with inflamed tumours in the legs.
rayed with the yellows Discoloured with jaundice.
fives Properly 'vives', glandular swellings under the jaws.
staggers Loss of balance.
begnawn with the bots Gnawed by worms.
swayed Strained, and so sagging in the backbone.
shoulder-shotten With a strained shoulder.

near-legged before Moving both front legs as near-legs, or possibly knock-kneed.
half-cheeked bit Bit with the rings broken or badly fitting.
headstall Part of the bridle fitted to the head.
sheep's leather i.e. of inferior quality.
restrained Pulled back.
to keep him from stumbling With his two near front legs?
girth Strap under the horse's belly.
pieced Mended by joining two pieces.
crupper The back part of a saddle fitted to carry a passenger.
velure Velvet.
two letters Two initials.
studs Brass nails.
packthread Twine.
Who comes with him? Wondering, if this be Petruchio, what his retinue can be like.
caparisoned Equipped.
stock Stocking.
kersey boot-hose Woollen stocking inside (riding) boot.
gartered Tied (at knee).
list Strip of cloth.
humour of forty fancies Obscure. A 'fancy' could be anything from a gay feather to a printed ditty, and both could be stuck in a hat.
pricked in't Pinned on to it.
footboy Page.
odd humour Strange mood.
pricks Urges.
oftentimes Tranio is drawing on his imagination.
all one Same thing.
hold Bet.
come not well i.e. not well-dressed.
you halt not You are not limping, as you would be if you were not 'coming well'.
Were it not better I should rush in thus Were it not better I should rush in like this than not at all?
wondrous monument Eye-catching structure erected to commemorate someone or something.
prodigy Amazing omen.
unprovided Badly turned out.
shame to your estate A disgrace to your social position.
enforced to digress Compelled to turn aside (from purchase of proper apparel).
excuse Give an explanation for.
what she will wear in me i.e. my body (and the character that goes with it).
bid good morrow Say good morning (of the day itself). 'Morrow' has come to mean the morning after.
seal the title i.e. take possession.

lovely Loving.
event Outcome.
to love concerneth . . . liking To Bianca's love (which it seems Lucentio has sometime before informed Tranio that he has won) it is essential that they (he and his master) add her father's approval, to be gained by a guarantee by someone acting as Vincentio of the settlement offered by 'Lucentio'.
your worship Speaking to him as his master. Perhaps humorously.
skills Matters.
fit him to our turn Get him to behave as we want him to.
Of greater sums Either Tranio was not exaggerating in his competition with Gremio, or Lucentio has tacitly allowed him to go on inventing.
quietly enjoy your hope Achieve your desire without further difficulty.
steal our marriage i.e. elope.
overreach Outrun.
narrow-prying Inquiring too closely into details, e.g. of the dowry.
quaint Skilled.
Signor Gremio Tranio, now they are no longer alone, speaks as 'Lucentio', and Lucentio listens respectfully as a tutor.
groom Man or manservant. The original meaning (from O. E. *guma*), but here used with contempt.
Curster than she? Tranio, for all his quick-wittedness, having failed to see the reason for Petruchio's recent masquerade ('He hath some meaning in his mad attire'), still thinks of Kate as a shrew.
Should ask i.e. came to that point in the marriage service.
by gogs-wouns By God's wounds (cf. 'zounds!').
if any list If anyone wants to.
for why Because.
cozen Cheat.
muscadel A wine, drunk at marriages.
sops Bread soaked in wine, but here probably the dregs.
hungerly Hungrily, i.e. without sufficient nourishment.
to ask him sops i.e. to ask Petruchio to give it the dregs.
clamorous Resounding.
parting i.e. of their lips.
rout Crowd.
to dine with me i.e. with me as a fellow-guest.
Make it no wonder Do not wonder at it.
I am content Deliberately ambiguous: he appears to 'agree', but is really 'gratified'.
But yet not stay Yet I will not stay.
The oats have eaten the horses Typical of Grumio, a jest at the mad scene being enacted.
your boots are green i.e. cleaned for a journey. A hint at departure.
a jolly surly groom An extremely surly husband. Ironic use of an old word with a variety of pleasant meanings; we still say 'jolly good', but no longer 'jolly rotten'.

take it . . . roundly Presume to behave so roughly to begin with.
to do To do with it.
stay my leisure Wait till I am ready.
now it begins to work Gremio is changing back to his opinion that Kate is the more masterful.
domineer Lord it.
look not big Don't be pompous.
stare Put on an indignant look.
my ox, my ass, my any thing Parodying the Tenth Commandment.
mine action Punning on a case in court and a fight.
buckler Shield.
Went they not quickly If they hadn't gone so quickly.
Petruchio is Kated i.e. matched by one with an equal temper.
supply Fill.

Revision questions on Act III

1 Describe the rivalry between the tutors Cambio and Licio.

2 Give an account of the wedding as reported by Gremio.

3 Can you condemn or justify Petruchio for the extravagance of his behaviour?

Act IV Scene 1

Grumio precedes his master home in order to have the fires lit because of the cold weather which has punished the travellers even worse than Petruchio's treatment of his bride. His fellow-servant, Curtis, who has got the house ready and instructed the other servants how to behave on this special occasion, is given a grim account of the journey.

The household are scarcely paraded when the newly married couple enter, Petruchio in a towering rage because his orders that they should be met in the park have not been carried out, Kate bedraggled and depressed, and venturing only mild protests. When the meal is laid before them, it is condemned as overdone mutton, bad for bad tempers, and thrown at the servers, after which Kate is hustled, still fasting, to the bedroom. The scared household reassemble briefly for Curtis to describe (for the audience's benefit) the 'curtain lecture' delivered by the bridegroom to a dazed bride, only to scatter again at his approach.

In soliloquy resembling the braggart speeches of the history plays Shakespeare was engaged on at this period, the Tamer of the Shrew lays bare his plan to 'kill a wife with kindness'. The 'kindness' is to be shown by pretending to do all in her interests; the 'killing' is to consist of starving her and robbing her of sleep. By now the taming exceeds in volubility and violence the shrewishness it has set out to cure: as so often, the remedy is worse than the disease!

Commentary

The half-frozen Grumio, sent ahead to ensure that a fire is lighted (for whose benefit?) in what should be a well-organized household, makes the audience shiver, even before he tells the tale, pretending all the while to withhold it – which reinforces the effect – of the terrible journey, made far more unendurable by Petruchio's continued bullying. After listening to the further catalogue of atrocities the sober Curtis sums up what is now in everybody's mind: 'he is more shrew than she'.

Kate's earlier tantrums now seem minor outbursts compared with Petruchio's unreasonably violent treatment of her and of everybody else. What was temperamental and spasmodic in her is now 'politic' and systematic in him. Ironically he professes to abstain from overdone meat to avoid attacks of 'choler'. The shrew is increasingly a helpless victim (at a time when women had fewer safeguards than today); her bitter feelings are partially transmuted into sympathy with those who are made to suffer as part of her cure. The cruelties of the journey which have been described in *retrospect* by Grumio are mirrored in those which are held in almost gleeful *prospect* by her husband.

The service, in an establishment wealthy enough to employ a retinue of servants, is made to appear as shabby as the clothes that were donned by the bridegroom; had they been as well-drilled as might have been expected, however, Petruchio would still have found fault. At this point one wonders whether his attitude has long been characteristic of him, thus explaining much that is amiss, or whether what we have seen has been assumed for the express purpose of subduing Katherina. There is a natural swagger, but does he deliberately inflict cruelty? Grumio could tell us.

Some minor discrepancies suggest that this is a play that Shakespeare put together in some haste. There is a confusing list of names: curiously the only servants declared fit to appear do *not* appear – Adam, Ralph and Gregory. 'Cousin Ferdinand' does not respond to the summons – either this is an oversight or he has wisely chosen to keep out of the way; the favourite spaniel has gone missing!

Fie, fie Grumio is in an unusually serious mood.
jades Poor horses.
rayed Muddied.
a little pot and soon hot i.e. more easily heated. Proverbial for a small, quick-tempered person.
But I . . . warm myself i.e. by my quick temper?
taller Here in the sense of greater stature, i.e. the higher the colder!
a run To start the slide with.
cast on no water The call of 'Fire!' would normally be followed by 'cast on more water!' Here the call is for the fire to be lit.
I am no beast Grumio has applied the general phrase 'man, woman and beast' to his master, mistress and himself (forgetting the horse). Then he addresses Curtis as 'fellow-servant', equating him, in Curtis's view, with a beast. Grumio may have intended it as an insult.
horn Symbol of a 'cuckold', a husband to whom his wife has been unfaithful.
cold comfort . . . hot office i.e. punishment for slackness in preparing a fire.
in every office but thine Doing anything but light a fire.
have thy duty Receive what is due to you.
'Jack, boy! ho, boy!' The first line in an old catch which ends in the word 'news', which may have brought it to Grumio's mind.
cony-catching Rabbit-catching, i.e. deceiving simple people. There is a pun on 'catch', continued by Grumio in 'catching' cold.
fustian Coarse cloth, worn by servants.
officer Servant.
Jacks Leather drinking-vessels, cleaned on the inside.
Jills Metal cups, polished on the outside.
carpets Coverings laid, not on the floor, but on tables and chairs.
sensible tale Pun on 'showing good sense' and 'that can be felt'.
knock at your ear Grumio associates knocking with physical assault (see II,1), but here, perhaps, he recollects Petruchio's expression 'knock me at this gate', something which expects a response (by someone listening).
Imprimis In the first place. Latin for the first item on a list.
crossed me i.e. asked a stupid question.
thou should'st have heard The tale that is being withheld as a retaliation is, as so often, nevertheless told.
bemoiled Soiled.
waded through the dirt i.e. after extricating herself from under the horse!
she prayed . . . before An assumption based on her character as a shrew, since he has known her only two days.
crupper Here a strap looped under the tail to hold the saddle in place.

things of worthy memory Incidents that would have been worth telling you about.
unexperienced Uninformed.
he is more shrew than she This may by now have also occurred to the audience.
What talk I of this? Why am I wasting time talking about it?
slickly Sleekly.
blue coats i.e. livery of servants.
of an indifferent knit Equally matched.
curtsy Now used only of women.
not presume . . . hands i.e. obeisance before grooming.
to countenance To show respect for.
a face of her own Feeble pun on 'countenance'.
credit Curtis changes the word to avoid the puns of Grumio and runs into another, on (1) the 'credit' which is based on reputation and (2) that on which money is borrowed.
Welcome home This group reception suggests a lengthy absence rather than a few days. At the start of I,2 Petruchio speaks of having just left Verona, not far from Padua.
spruce Smart.
Cock's passion God's passion. The comedian is scared out of his wits.
as I was before Pun on the two functions of 'before': time and place.
swain Rustic (a meaning already conveyed in 'peasant').
whoreson malt-horse drudge Beastly driver of a horse on a malthouse treadmill.
unpink'd With no small ornamental holes pricked in the leather.
link Material from 'links' (torches) used as blacking for hats.
sheathing Having its scabbard renewed.
Adam, Ralph and Gregory These properly dressed servants remain off-stage.
'Where is the life that late I led?' A line from a lost ballad, referring to former bachelor days.
Where are those i.e. the servants ordered to bring in the supper.
Why, when Expressing impatience.
orders grey Franciscans.
mend the plucking of the other Make a better job of pulling the other off.
Shall I have some water? Am I going to get some water or not?
will you let it fall? You *would* drop it.
a fault unwilling i.e. he did not mean to.
beetle-headed Thick-headed. A 'beetle' was a heavy mallet.
you have a stomach Possible pun on hunger and temper.
dresser A sideboard.
trenchers Flat boards on which meat was served.
heedless joltheads Clumsy blockheads.
with you straight Even with you at once.
well, if you were so contented Good, if you had a mind to accept it.
engenders choler Creates bile (the 'humour' for bad temper).

of ourselves . . . choleric As far as we are concerned, we are both bad-tempered.
't shall be mended i.e. there will be an improvement (in conditions here).
in her own humour By displaying the same bad temper.
rates Scolds.
politicly Of set purpose. By revealing his plans, as in his first soliloquy (II,1), Petruchio provides the audience with a picture of what Kate is having to endure.
sharp Hungry.
stoop Swoop down. In Kate's case, 'obey her master'.
lure Bait used to lure the falcon down.
man my haggard Tame my wild hawk. A play on 'man'.
watch her Keep her awake.
kites Hawks.
bate and beat Flutter and flap.
meat Food.
nor none Double negative used for emphasis, as also in next line.
I intend I shall declare.
watch Be awake.
kill a wife with kindness A drastically literal use of 'kill' instead of the metaphorical meaning 'ruin' or 'spoil'.
better how Does this mean 'of a gentler way'?
'tis charity to show i.e. kindness (to the shrew or to the audience?) by demonstrating it. The rhyme indicates the contemporary pronunciation of 'shrew'.

Act IV Scene 2

Hortensio leads Tranio, whom he knows only as 'Lucentio', to a spot where they can observe the real Lucentio making love to Bianca. Tranio pretends shocked amazement and when the indignant Hortensio reveals he is no mere tutor but of genteel status, the cunning servant draws him on into a joint renunciation of the lady. Hortensio then leaves in search of his second string, a wealthy widow. Tranio approaches the happy couple with the news of Hortensio's and 'his own' change of heart.

Biondello arrives to announce to his 'master' (both are present) his discovery of an old schoolmaster suitable to take on the role of Vincentio. The lovers leave Tranio, their all-purpose manager, to examine the Pedant and persuade him to play Vincentio in order to impose on Baptista and get the marriage settlement signed (by a man with no wealth to bestow and no son to inherit any). He does this by frightening the old man with a pretended state of hostilities between his city of Mantua and

Padua, where he now finds himself; the Pedant is only too grateful to adopt a disguise for his own safety and is ready in return to stand surety for his rescuer's ability as his 'son' to support a wife.

Commentary

Now undeceived as to Bianca's real affection, Hortensio reveals his superficiality by swiftly substituting for her the rich widow he has been holding in reserve, and by leaving Padua to pay a return visit to his friend Petruchio at his 'taming school'; thus the inconvenience to the plot of his discovering who his partner in the renunciation of Bianca really is before the final scene of reconciliation is avoided.

Tranio further loyally serves his master by practising a deception (on a prospective father-in-law) that would be unworthy of the youthful heir to a fortune who has just won for himself a beautiful heiress. When, however, he tells the Pedant 'My father is here look'd for every day' this invention is to prove truer than he could have imagined.

The sub-plot by now is so involved that the average spectator would be as unlikely to attempt to sort out the various relationships as would Sly himself, were he still among the *dramatis personae*, but *his* disentanglement (or disillusionment) is now of less than academic interest.

Lucentio Here meaning himself.
bears me fair in hand Encourages me.
what I have said Hortensio has told Tranio what he has observed between Bianca and Lucentio.
resolve Answer.
the Art to Love *Ars Amatoria* by Ovid.
quick proceeders Fast learners. Probably a sarcastic pun on the university expression, 'proceed' from BA to MA.
despiteful Spiteful.
wonderful A matter for wonder (that Bianca should be so guilty of double-dealing).
such a one as leaves a gentleman i.e. a maiden who turns from himself.
makes a god of such a cullion i.e. adores a mere tutor. A 'cullion' is a wretch.
lightness Disloyalty.
Forswear Give up, swear to have nothing to do with.
favours Kindnesses.
fondly Foolishly.

unfeigned Without pretence, genuine. This costs Tranio no regrets.
beastly Like an animal.
proud disdainful haggard More appropriate to Bianca's sister, who is being treated by Hortensio's friend Petruchio as if she were one (end of IV,1).
ta'en you napping Caught you in the act.
gentle love Spoken in his part of 'official' wooer.
Tranio, you jest She knows now, from Lucentio, who he is.
rid of Licio Lucentio's acquaintance with Hortensio has been mainly as the tutor with the lute.
eleven and twenty long This makes the thirty-one of the card-game in I,2,33, but those are pips, not tricks. Eleven and Twenty has also been traced to 'eleven score', a favourite term for an enormous number.
an ancient angel An old man of the right stamp (from the gold coin, the 'angel', which had the archangel Michael on one side). Or, perhaps, an angel from heaven, descended in time to rescue them.
mercatante Merchant (obsolete Ital.).
pedant Schoolmaster.
like a father The average Elizabethan in his fifties would look like an 'ancient'.
what of him, Tranio? What do you think of him (as my father)? Lucentio leaves his trusty servant with the hard work.
my tale i.e. the deception he is about to practise on the Pedant.
What countryman? From what country are you?
that goes hard i.e. my life is difficult enough.
stay'd Held under arrest.
it i.e. death.
worse for me than so i.e. worse for me than you make out.
courtesy A kindness.
this I will advise you I will give you further information about my proposition.
To save your life Did Tranio get this idea from his own disguise as Lucentio? The reason given by Lucentio to Biondello (I,1,233) for the change of costume was 'to save my life . . . I killed a man'.
for his sake For Vincentio's sake, who may not be in time to sign the guarantee!
credit Financial standing.
undertake Assume.
take upon you Play your part.
repute you Regard you as.
pass assurance Sign a deed of guarantee.
to clothe you i.e. as a prosperous merchant instead of a schoolmaster.

Act IV Scene 3

After a sleepless night with nothing to eat Katherina deepens the pathos gathering round her by her own account of her treatment, in which she draws a sad contrast between the peace and comfort of the home she has so often disturbed by her quarrelsome outbreaks and the sheer discomfort and noisy accusations which now surround her. When Grumio teases her by offering her a taste of mustard instead of the beef itself (which induces 'choler') she gives him in a flash of her old temper what must appear to the audience a well-deserved beating.

In the following episode clothing replaces food as the instrument of torture. We see more clearly Petruchio's method of taming a turbulent spirit: it is to pretend to understand the opposite of what is said or done. Whatever is good or desirable is bad, or even an evil influence. A neat cap is derided as too small for her, and she is praised for 'rejecting' it, while promised such a model once she has become 'gentle'. The criticism of the gown, apparently a fashionable 'creation', runs to extraordinary lengths, mainly a triangular dispute brought on by the tailor's bold 'arrogance' in refuting Petruchio's switching of pronouns from Katherina's 'you mean' (l.104) and then defending his workmanship by reference to the terms of the 'order'. The quibbling is mostly too feeble to be genuine Shakespeare, for example Grumio's assertion that the 'cuts' (presumably fashionable slashes) were made only to be sewn up again. Here, as elsewhere, Grumio serves as his master's proxy: the diminutive servant confronts the conventionally small stature of a tailor, derived from his being bent over his work.

Having made extreme use of irrational contradiction in such domestic matters as food and clothes, Petruchio comes to an equally unreasonable decision to return to Kate's home so soon after leaving it (on a similar outrageous impulse). Yet it is she who, merely questioning the exact time of their proposed arrival, is accused of *persistently* 'crossing' him.

Commentary

This scene is undoubtedly the climax of the play. The bitter relish to Petruchio's quite phenomenal ill-treatment is his brazen pretence to be showing her the devoted love of a newly wedded husband.

The brisk dispute between husband and wife over the cap, allowing time for an elaborate preparation of the gown for presentation, is followed by a different kind of altercation to which Katherina contributes all she has to say in three lines.

I dare not This reply (a refusal of food) to a request off-stage brings the characters onto the scene, the starving Kate in pursuit of something, anything, to appease her hunger.
my wrong Wrong done to me.
present alms Immediate charity.
with brawling fed Fed with angry words instead of food.
spites me Angers me.
As who should say . . . death As if to declare that by keeping me from sleeping or eating he is saving me from some fatal disease or sudden death.
neat's foot Ox's or calf's foot.
too choleric The cause of too much bile (cf. IV,1,159). Grumio is obviously acting on his master's instructions, not some foolery of his own. Ungrateful, nevertheless, in view of her gallant attempts to save him from a beating on their way to the house.
I cannot tell I cannot say for certain.
the very name of meat The bare mention of food. Here she takes to beating him!
all amort Mortified.
dress thy meat Prepare your food.
is sorted to no proof Have turned out to be in vain. 'Pains' in the sense of 'effort' attracts the singular verb.
I thank you, sir Spoken humbly?
Kate, eat apace Is he urging her to compete with Hortensio or telling her to be quick over it as the tailor is waiting?
farthingales Hooped skirts.
double change of bravery Two changes of fine clothes.
knavery Nonsense.
ruffling Ruffled, gaily fashioned.
What news with you, sir? Turning from tailor to haberdasher (supplier of hats).
bespeak Order. The verb survives in 'bespoke tailor'.
cockle The shell-fish.
knack Knick-knack, toy.
trick Another word for 'toy'.
This doth fit the time This is in the fashion.
When you are gentle Pun on 'mild-mannered' and 'well-bred' (a gentle woman).
Your betters . . . mind Better men than you have put up with my frank words. This spark of resistance is needed to justify the ordeal to follow.
thou say'st true As if Kate's piece of defiance had been nothing but criticism of the 'cap'.
custard-coffin Container for custard, such as pie-crust.
masquing stuff Costume for actors in a masque, i.e. not proper clothes.
demi-cannon Small gun with a bore of about six inches.
like to a censer The comparison is to the perforations in the top of a brazier used in Italian shops to purify the air and warm clothes.

neither cap nor gown The haberdasher has taken the cap with him.
mar it to the time Spoil it for the sake of fashion. Merely substituting 'mar' for 'make'.
hop me over every kennel Jump over every street gutter (then in the middle of the street).
make your best of it Do what you can with it – for another customer.
quaint Skilfully made.
he means to make a puppet of thee Petruchio still acts as if in defence of his bride and treats Kate's 'you' as addressed to the tailor and not to himself. This the tailor ventures to correct and draws upon himself a torrent of abuse. A puppet (Fr. *poupée*) was a dressed-up doll.
thou thread Petruchio throws every tailoring term at the unfortunate man, even associated insects (the cricket's chirp would be monotonous in winter, as the tailor stitched away).
nail One-sixteenth of a yard.
Brav'd Defied.
quantity Small portion.
bemete Measure, i.e. strike. Cf. Grumio's challenge below, l.150.
think on prating Reflect on the error of talking wildly.
whil'st thou liv'st For the rest of your life.
deceived Mistaken.
had direction Was given orders.
Grumio gave order This makes the argument three-cornered, with Hortensio keeping contact with the world of sanity and Kate a dumb witness to this increasingly far-fetched and vulgar dispute over the gown she is obviously not going to be allowed to wear.
faced Having facings or trimmings. The pun in 'Face not me' (don't confront me) is doubled with one on 'brave' with similar meanings: (1) dressed up in fine clothes, (2) challenge.
note of the fashion Written instructions on the fashion to be followed.
lies in's throat Lies deliberately (deep).
if he say If it says.
Imprimis In the first place.
loose-bodied gown An allusion to the garb of prostitutes.
bottom Reel (spool or bobbin) on which thread is wound.
compassed Round-edged.
trunk sleeve i.e. padded, like the 'trunk hose' of the period.
curiously Carefully or elaborately.
I'll prove upon thee A duelling threat.
and I had thee . . . where If I had you in a suitable place.
for thee straight Ready for you now.
bill Pun on the note and a weapon.
mete-yard Yardstick.
no odds Nothing in his favour.
the gown is not for me I do not wish to buy it.
unto thy master's use To make what he can of it (cf. l.100).
conceit Witty idea.
habiliments Affected word for 'clothes'.

proud i.e. through spending little.
furniture Outfit.
lay it on me Blame me.
frolic Be gay. A cruel request.
There will we mount, and thither walk on foot The inverted order has, perhaps, some significance. Petruchio refers first to their mounting their horses (presumably better steeds than that which brought him to the wedding) at Long-lane End, and then, disappointingly, announces that they will make their way there – on foot. This, while the horses are being walked there also!
dinner-time Then eleven o'clock. Supper was between six and seven. Petruchio's country house (IV,1) is an unknown distance from Baptista's house in Padua, but walking is going to take up a fair part of the four hours.
It shall be seven i.e. in the evening.
You are still crossing it You persist in thwarting me.
ere I do The perverse accuser of perversity here contradicts himself.

Act IV Scene 4

Tranio appears outside Baptista's house, bringing with him the old schoolmaster, now dressed like a rich merchant and given some details of Vincentio's past, such as a casual meeting with Baptista some years before in an inn in Genoa. Biondello comes out, having announced to Baptista, on Tranio's instructions, that Vincentio is expected by his son to arrive from Venice.

Baptista issues from the house accompanied by the said son (as the tutor 'Cambio'), who remains quietly in the background watching his man Tranio acquit himself in what should be his place. The Pedant turns to Baptista and, rather pedantically, offers him a marriage agreement between 'their' children. Baptista is quite impressed by the substitute Vincentio (the original being known to him only 'by report', II,1,104) and readily agrees to draw up a mutual settlement. However, he prefers somewhere else than his own house, where Gremio is still lurking and might jealously resent the success of the 'richer' rival. When Tranio suggests his (i.e. Lucentio's) lodging, they all set out for it, after Baptista has despatched 'Cambio' (of all people) to bring Bianca. Tranio, using Biondello to deliver the message, advises Lucentio to get married *before* the signing of the contract, which may well be prevented by the discovery of the impersonation of Vincentio.

Biondello discharges his errand in his usual flippant way by 'expounding' in stages: (1) Baptista has been decoyed away on a false ceremony; (2) Lucentio is to bring Bianca to the festivity;

but (3) a priest is waiting at a nearby church (that is, as soon as Biondello has gone to warn him!). When Lucentio enquires what all this adds up to, Biondello, with pun, Latin tag, rhyming couplet and analogy, advises him (over his shoulder, as he must rejoin the others) to seize his opportunity – elope with Bianca and get married without her father's permission.

Commentary

A scene of dissimulation and intrigue if ever there was one, with added confusion from doubtful stage directions. The only characters who appear as themselves are Baptista and Biondello. The Pedant, incidentally, makes a confident job of the imposture *imposed* on him – Elizabethan schoolmasters, like some of their modern successors, acted in and produced plays.

The dialogue is as mediocre as the action, which in two respects at least is artificially contrived: (1) the change of house and (2) Tranio's communication with his master, guarded with such precautions that, added to the disguises, they have led to varying textual versions and wrongly attributed speeches. The important line is 'I pray the gods she may with all my heart', which must be Lucentio's and not Biondello's (a gay spark hardly likely to be so moved): thus it follows naturally on the previous line. But then we are uncertain whether (1) Lucentio leaves ahead of the others, in which case he is shortly overtaken by Biondello somewhere on the way to Bianca, or (2) he pretends to leave (is 'get thee gone' addressed to him or to Lucentio?) but hides (behind some stage piece) from the others and is called out of hiding by Biondello when the coast is clear, or (3) since the scene is outside Baptista's house, neither has left the stage, but both remain: 'he has left me here behind' explains the page, elaborating Tranio's earlier dumb-show with (time-consuming) hints to Lucentio to get married post-haste. Our playwright must also have forgotten that the lover who seems so slow in comprehending the message actually made the suggestion himself to Tranio in III,2,138. But such minor incongruities in a bustling comedy do not call for comment, except that with the departure of Hortensio there is no other purpose in this elaborate subterfuge than to deceive old Baptista and present him with a *fait accompli*.

Lucentio seems on stage rather shy of his new-found love and needs to be jerked into action by the cheeky Biondello; his tardiness, as if overwhelmed by her beauty, poses a clear contrast with Petruchio's overwhelming way with feminine resistance!

please it you A French construction, *plait-il?*
but I be deceiv'd Unless I am mistaken. Another French construction.
the Pegasus An inn with a familiar name in England. There was one in the Inner Temple, of which the *pegasus*, a winged horse, is the heraldic device.
austerity Severity (of tone).
school'd Thoroughly briefed. The Pedant knows Biondello only as the page who introduced him.
Now do your duty This cryptic expression has only one possible meaning: to inform Lucentio about the arrangements made for him, and told him below by Biondello.
Tut, fear not me He has certainly had some practice in imagining Tranio as his master, Lucentio.
a tall fellow In modern parlance, 'Good man!'
hold thee that to drink Giving him a tip.
Give me Bianca for my patrimony If this means anything, it must be this: Settle my patrimony on me now and so enable me to win Bianca for my wife.
Soft Take it easy.
stay Delay.
to like To like it.
curious Particular (in my enquiries).
shortness Conciseness.
dissemble deeply their affections Hide their real love for others.
pass Convey in legal form to.
affied Engaged.
assurance Guarantee.
with either part's agreement stand Prove agreeable to both parties.
hearkening Listening (for an opportunity).
happily By chance.
pass the business Settle the matter.
Send for your daughter by your servant here This can only refer to Cambio (Lucentio).
My boy shall fetch the scrivener This can only refer to Biondello. A scrivener would draw up the contracts of marriage.
It likes me well If so, then he must next say, 'Cambio, hie you home', and not 'Biondello', as some versions have it.
pittance Originally a small amount of food provided, out of 'piety', to a monastery.
I pray the gods . . . heart This must be spoken by Lucentio, as it underlines the extraordinary irony of the previous line uttered by Baptista.
Dally not with the gods Tranio shows characteristic impatience with his master's pious utterance and hastens him on his way to Bianca.

Perhaps it is here that he winks and laughs at him, as recalled a few lines below.
One mess One course.
your cheer The hospitality extended to you.
better it in Pisa When 'Lucentio' is in his own home.
my master Biondello is the go-between for his counterfeit master and the real one, and he gets his fun calling Lucentio 'Cambio' and speaking of Tranio as 'master'.
moralize them Explain the 'moral', i.e. the meaning, of them.
deceiving father of a deceitful son There is a fine verbal distinction here between the Pedant playing his part and the servant playing the part of his master, but adding to it a trick of his own.
The old priest . . . at all hours This arrangement (yet to be made) is Tranio's idea, his master having no time for anything but adoring his Bianca.
cum privilegio ad imprimendum solum Low Latin for 'with the right to be the sole printer'.
to come against you come with your appendix To come to meet you and your lady, about to be joined to you – like an 'appendix', a printing term which expresses the subordinate position held by the conventional wife of the day.
roundly go about her Go straightaway in search of her.

Act IV Scene 5

Petruchio and Kate, accompanied by Hortensio and servants, are quite unnecessarily labouring on foot across country to reach her father's house in Padua. When he mischievously refers to the moon, she counters by declaring it is the sun. Angered by such contradiction, he calls off the horses until she agrees it is the moon (or whatever he likes to call it) and changes back to the sun when he does. Not content with this victory, he greets a portly merchant, who has just appeared, as a fair young maiden and bids Kate do likewise. When she obediently does so, she is rebuked for such mad behaviour – and humbly apologizes.

Learning that the newcomer's name is Vincentio, Petruchio welcomes him as a 'father', claiming the relationship through the very recent marriage of Vincentio's 'son' to the sister of his wife Kate. The rather startled old man takes some reassuring that this relationship thus thrust upon him is not as bogus as the manner in which he was first spoken to.

Commentary

The scenes in this act have so far alternated between Petruchio's house in Verona and Baptista's in Padua, some forty miles apart. Now that matters have been more or less settled in both places – Baptista having agreed to the marriage of Bianca to Lucentio (still represented by Tranio), and his other daughter having little left of her shrewishness – we are back on the open road, not as seen through the eyes of Grumio, but in grim reality. Instead of foul weather this time the sun shines brightly, but Petruchio is as contradictory as ever, while pouncing on his wife for contradicting him.

Come on . . . once more This suggests difficult travelling or sheer weariness after an hour or more on foot. Or is it plain lagging behind?
our father's Baptista's house.
It is not moonlight now Either she has not learnt anything from the dispute over the time of day, or she is making one more desperate effort to assert herself.
fetch our horses back again i.e. from the point (Long-lane End) where they were to mount for the main part of the journey.
rush-candle A rush in fat. A flickering light.
then you lie To have to contradict your own knowingly false assertion is one of the lowest forms of humiliation.
so it shall be so for Katherina Final surrender, but the ordeal is not yet over.
go thy ways i.e. the battle is over and won and you may go home.
war of white and red i.e. alternate paling and flushing. An allusion to the campaigns between the French (lilies) and the English (roses).
Happy the parents . . . bed-fellow Adapted from Ovid.
This is a man The trick is now applied to a living instead of an inanimate object.
so bedazzled with the sun A sly reference to the previous argument.
green Pun on (1) the effect of too much sun and (2) youth.
a reverend father The respectable head of a family.
by this By now.
qualified Possessing qualities.
beseem Become, befit.
pleasant Joking. Vincentio fears a second trick may be played on him.
jealous Suspicious.
Have to Now for.
untoward Awkward.

Revision questions on Act IV

1 Describe the two different ways in which Bianca is being courted.

2 Give an account, as Katherina might tell it, of her experiences in this act.

3 What various parts are played in this act by servants and craftsmen?

Act V Scene 1

Biondello, having warned the priest to be ready, has returned to guide Lucentio and Bianca to the church for their secret wedding. He determines to wait till he sees them wed before going back to Tranio who is in his (i.e. Lucentio's) house, entertaining Baptista and the Pedant (posing as Vincentio) for the purpose of getting the sham marriage agreement signed. The scene is the street in front of the house.

Petruchio and his wife, together with the real Vincentio, encounter Gremio hovering outside; the old man is unaware that Bianca and her lover have just flitted past. Vincentio persuades Petruchio, before he goes on to Baptista's house, to step into his son's lodging. Such is the sound of revelry within that Gremio sarcastically bids them knock louder. Instead of the door being opened to Vincentio, the Pedant looks through the window and speaks as if to unwelcome intruders. When it transpires that there are two Vincentios, Petruchio (fallible for once) suspects his fellow-traveller rather than the man who has been received into the house, while the Pedant, determined to play his part to the last, calls for his arrest.

At this point Vincentio finds a sudden and discomforting clue to the riddle in the returning Biondello, who brazenly recognizes only the old man at the window as his master. This results in a beating, and his cries for help bring the party within down into the street. Tranio (in Lucentio's clothes) impudently demands Vincentio's name. Outraged by this second refusal by one of his household to acknowledge him, Vincentio declares he has known this 'Lucentio' since he was three. When the Pedant asserts that Tranio is 'Lucentio', heir to himself, 'Vincentio', the old man fears his son has been murdered and his identity assumed by Tranio. He calls for Tranio's arrest and is himself arrested by a constable. Here Gremio intervenes, declaring that he believes the stranger to be Vincentio, but lamely conceding that Tranio must be Lucentio.

To cut the knot of all this confusion, the real Lucentio enters with his newly wedded wife and Biondello, who rapidly disappears, accompanied by the two other hired conspirators. The young couple ask forgiveness of their respective parents, and some rather unconvincing explanations are offered. The two fathers enter the house to sort the matter out, followed by Lucentio and Bianca in some trepidation. Meanwhile, the other couple, who have found entertainment in all this violent altercation, turn to enter in the wake of the others, but not before Petruchio has demanded, and received, a kiss there and then in the open street, and has expressed his delight and admiration for his 'tamed falcon'.

Commentary

The tangled web of deceit, started by Lucentio and extended by Tranio, here reaches its greatest confusion, fathers and sons, masters and servants being interchanged and the whole well-sustained by the Pedant and the page, and indeed Tranio himself. The amazing riddle confronting Vincentio is quickly solved, as Lucentio and Bianca, warned by Biondello (who has had to improvise at the unexpected sight of his real master from home) kneel before the two old men. Baptista finds difficulty in comprehending that Cambio is not Cambio, and Vincentio is determined to punish his servant Tranio for nearly sending him to prison.

Thus this second marriage, which might have been expected to prove an anti-climax after the whirlwind affair of Petruchio and Katherina, has provided the audience with some excitement; at the feast in celebration of it the late shrew and her tamer are welcome as guests, not as principals (they were absentees from their own wedding banquet). Katherina looks on placidly at the turmoil attending her sister's betrothal!

Three old men are closely involved in the action. If Shakespeare ever modelled any of his aged characters on his father, would it have been one of these?

out before Ahead of the others (and therefore not seeing them).
I marvel Cambio comes not Is he waiting for information about how Bianca has reacted to his tutor's reading of Ovid?
my father's The house of his father-in-law, Baptista.
bears Lies (in the sense of direction). Cf. 'bearing'.
some cheer is toward Vincentio can hear sounds of the company enjoying themselves.
so long as I live While I am alive as his (pretended) father.
frivolous circumstances Petty details.
good shipping A good journey.
crack-hemp Rascal who will strain the hangman's rope; gallows-bird.
choose Select my form of execution.

notorious Infamous.
see where he looks out of the window Biondello has been so thoroughly 'schooled' that he chooses to recognize the Pedant instead of his own master.
Help, son! Calling on Tranio.
let's stand aside Hero and heroine replace Sly, forming a more interested audience; not unlike the lovers, reconciled after their quarrels, looking on in *A Midsummer Night's Dream*, Act V.
what are you? This extraordinary refusal to recognize his master, thus supporting Biondello, is, of course, farcical.
copatain hat A high, conical-shaped hat.
husband Economical manager.
spend all If the servant dresses thus, what extravagant attire will his son be wearing?
be forthcoming Is produced when his case comes for trial.
cony-catched Easily tricked.
haled Hauled about.
O we are spoiled – and yonder he is The plot is ruined: there is the real Vincentio.
deny him An extraordinary request to his master, begging him to decline to recognize his own father.
Lives my sweet son? He is relieved to find Lucentio has not been murdered.
How hast thou offended? Baptista sees only his daughter with her tutor 'Cambio'.
While counterfeit supposes blear'd thine eyne A bland confession to having tricked his future father-in-law in order to marry Bianca without his permission. No wonder that there are now two outraged fathers. 'Blear'd', i.e. what he saw was not the real thing. For a possible allusion in 'supposes' see *Sources*.
packing Scheming.
brav'd Defied.
is not this my Cambio? Baptista's old mind does not adapt itself readily to the whirligigs of this plot. It needs his daughter's solemn assurance that 'Cambio' the tutor is now what the vanished Tranio was.
Love wrought these miracles The master of languages is given to pretty generalities and metaphors like 'wished haven'.
I'll slit the villain's nose A recognized act of vengeance. The threat is to Tranio, the disrespectful servant.
we will content you We will smooth over the marriage.
sound the depth of Get to the bottom of. Baptista's use of 'knavery', which distresses his daughter, is another indication of his slowness in accepting a novel situation.
My cake is dough My suit has failed.
let's home again A much milder threat and not seriously meant, for their understanding is made clear in this charming end of scene.
Is not this well? i.e. see what a fine thing my wife's submission is.

Better once than never, for never too late A comical compound from 'Better late than never' and 'It is never too late to mend'.

Act V Scene 2

A final ensemble at a 'banquet' (in which conversation flows during the service of light refreshments). The whole cast is present and is welcomed by Lucentio as the host in a sober, reflective mood. Then follows a battle of wits (or rather three brief contests) in which the weapons are dubious puns, and in which all three women join, in the order: the Widow, Kate and Bianca. After this the ladies withdraw, leaving husbands, fathers and disappointed suitors to practise witticisms on one another. This leads to a challenge by Petruchio to the other husbands (Hortensio qualifies as such without any mention of his wedding!) with a wager on which wife will respond quickest to a summons. The stake is raised to a hundred crowns, and the confident Lucentio offers to try first. Biondello is asked to *bid* Bianca come. Her reply is that she is busy!

Hortensio, shocked by such a message, thinks it prudent to *entreat* the Widow. This time the lady refuses to come in answer to an obvious joke. Let him come to her! The scoffing Petruchio thereupon sends his own messenger (Grumio instead of Biondello) to *command* Kate to come.

The tamed shrew appears promptly and is equally promptly sent back to bring her gossiping companions with her, and to whip them in if they refuse to come. To his amazed fellow-men Petruchio triumphantly proclaims that Kate's behaviour testifies to the true love and the peaceful existence which obtain under the rule of a rightful master. Baptista, staggered by her transformation, adds large sums to the bet already made, as if giving away a fresh dowry for another, quite different, daughter. Petruchio caps this by promising a further achievement to deserve his winnings. When the three duly appear, he orders Kate to throw her cap on the ground and tread on it, which she does, to the disgust of the other two. Thereupon Petruchio bids his wife explain their duties to them.

Kate's monologue, on the desirability of complete obedience by the weaker woman to her guardian husband, is the longest speech in the play. The reception hoped for by a company of actors – a round of hearty applause – was sometimes solicited by a set epilogue: Kate's set terms, sounding rather as if dictated by someone, are more of a prologue – to a happier marital relationship. Actually the dialogue following it is so feeble that one suspects that it was not expected to be audible through the chorus of masculine cheers and feminine counter-cheers that would greet the end of the former shrew's Hymn to Husbands.

The audience to her performance disperse severally, leaving the producer to decide on the most suitable way of removing that other audience aloft – perhaps returning him to his real self – if, indeed, he is still there!

Commentary

The 'banquet' follows some 'great and good cheer', something more satisfying than the hasty 'pittance' rashly promised by Tranio for the contract; it actually disgusts Petruchio, whose cavalier attitude to meals has been vigorously demonstrated. 'Nothing but sit and sit, and eat and eat' is his comment. Nothing more has been heard of the justifiable suspicions aroused in the minds of Baptista and Vincentio in the last scene: there is room only for the social banter, from which emerges the most fantastic trick of all, in which Petruchio displays his tamed but beautiful falcon soaring, as he would see it, to a climax: in the triangular competition to find the least shrewish of the three wives, the first cannot come, the second will not, the third obeys promptly and utterly; her obedience is further demonstrated in climax form – to fetch the other wives, to throw her cap on the ground, and, crowning miracle, to lecture the others on submission to husbands.

This renunciation of shrewishness is couched for the most part in flexible, idiomatic and rhythmic verse, an early foretaste of the eloquence of a Portia or a Viola. The mediocrity of the final couplets may serve to indicate the origin of several inferior passages in the play: they were probably taken over uncritically from the earlier version. They are, indeed, an unfitting anti-climax to what has been a lively and entertaining comedy.

our jarring notes agree Our disputes are settled. Lucentio, once more master in his own house, indulges his vein of oratory.

overblown Blown over.

My banquet is to close our stomachs up . . . cheer A rather clinical invitation to the fruit, sweetmeats and wine which were consumed after the main meal, often in a different room.

Nothing but sit and sit, and eat and eat! Is this a good-humoured jest at the bounty provided, or a portent of a restless spirit, rendered impatient by the lengthy process of dining? He had a rough way with prepared meals in his own home.

nothing but what is kind Petruchio's complimentary reference to *both* daughters of Baptista has a pun on (1) generosity and (2) good-temper. It starts off another bout of punning.
For both our sakes i.e. his own and Petruchio's. Does Hortensio wish his widow were as amenable as the reformed Kate?
Hortensio fears his widow An English linguistic trait of using often the same form of the verb for active and passive, hence ambiguity. The Widow takes it in the active sense and protests she is not frightened by him.
You are very sensible . . . sense i.e. 'you are a sensible woman not to be afraid of him' (spoken by the Shrew-tamer!) 'but I meant Hortensio is afraid of you.'
He that is giddy . . . round i.e. the sufferer thinks his symptoms are caused by something outside himself. The Widow gives her real meaning below.
Roundly replied A blunt answer. Another pun.
how mean you that? What is the meaning of that remark?
Thus I conceive by him i.e. that is my conception of his meaning in saying 'Hortensio is afeard of you'.
Conceives by me Is made pregnant by me. There is no delicacy in a punning contest!
conceives her tale Interprets her own statement.
I pray you Kate's *shrewd* mind is not fobbed off by this word-play. She suspects a reference to herself.
Measures . . . woe Calculates what he thinks my husband is suffering by what he himself suffers. 'He that is giddy' is Petruchio married to a shrew, and 'thinks the world turns round' is his belief that Hortensio is likewise scared of his wife.
mean meaning Paltry idea.
I mean you i.e. *you* are my mean meaning.
I am mean, indeed, respecting you Either (1) I am *spiteful* where you are concerned, or (2) I am *moderate* in my language when referring to you.
To her Go for her.
put her down Get the mastery over her.
my office My duty (as a husband).
Ha' to thee Here's to you.
butt Encounter one another (like goats).
Head and butt Head and tail (cf. 'butt-end').
hasty-witted body A quick-witted but unreflecting person.
horn Symbol of a betrayed husband.
awaken'd you The demure Bianca has hitherto sat silent beside her equally silent husband.
not frighted me A reference to the Widow's remarks.
Have at you . . . two i.e. I'm taking you on in a contest of wits; 'bitter', shrewd.
Am I your bird? Am I the game you are after?

shift my bush Flit to another covert. The ladies are about to withdraw, leaving the gentlemen to their own devices.
pursue . . . bow i.e. aiming and moving at the same time.
You are welcome all A bride's courtesy in her own home. Not an invitation to follow.
prevented me Got there (or away) first.
this bird you aim'd at i.e. you were a suitor to Bianca.
slipp'd Unleashed, unfastened for the chase. Used of hounds.
swift simile Punning on the quickness of the retort and the speed of a greyhound.
currish Like a cur. Further pun on the greyhound.
for yourself i.e. without the aid of a hound.
deer Punning on 'deer' and 'dear'.
I thank thee for that gird Lucentio seems to be expressing gratitude to Tranio for his comparison of himself hunting a deer with a dog (Tranio) with Petruchio hunting his deer without one. Lucentio and Tranio are both unaware of the change in the Shrew, though she has, indeed, just shown something of her old spirit.
gird Stroke of wit.
galled Rubbed against my skin.
glance away Rebound.
maimed you two outright Wounded both (Lucentio and Hortensio) fatally.
in good sadness In all seriousness.
the veriest shrew The most outright shrew. Baptista has still to discover the change in his daughter.
for assurance To make certain.
venture so much of Bet so much on.
twenty times Petruchio is justifiably proud of his newly trained falcon.
I'll be your half Put up half the money. After all, it was his comment on the shrewishness he still associates with Kate that prompted Petruchio's challenge.
she is busy Bianca's brief contribution to the witty exchanges has prepared us for this exhibition of independence.
entreat my wife Hortensio is hedging his bet.
some goodly jest This widow is being merry at her husband's expense. Up to now the three ladies have probably anticipated some such trick and jointly prepared for it. However, the case of Kate is a special one.
worse and worse The first was a transparent excuse, the second is open defiance.
the fouler fortune mine So much the worse for me.
by my holidame A strong oath expressing his astonishment ('holidame' meaning holiness).
Swinge me them Beat them.
An awful rule and right supremacy A rule that inspires awe or deep respect, and a (masculine) supremacy which is according to nature.
fair befall thee May good luck come your way (and he is about to bring it).

add unto their losses i.e. the mere two hundred crowns they have forfeited to Petruchio.
another daughter i.e. a different person.
froward The epithet once used of Kate.
womanly persuasion Corresponding in forcefulness to his manly persuasion on the wedding day.
I would your duty were as foolish too I wish your sense of duty to me had been equally foolish (and saved me a hundred crowns!).
laying Betting.
unkind Cruel.
Confounds thy name Destroys your reputation.
mov'd In a temper.
thick i.e. like soup.
one that cares for thee Petruchio's phrase.
To watch the night Spend the night watching (as she had been made to do).
honest will Upright decision.
simple Foolish.
unapt Unadapted.
conditions Characteristics.
unable Physically weak.
big Ambitious.
That seeming to be most which we indeed least are Not as strong as we would make out.
vail your stomachs Damp down your anger.
no boot In vain.
may it do him ease If it should help him.
a good hearing Good to hear. Similarly, 'a harsh hearing'. The play ends in some poor diction.
sped Finished.
white Of a bull's eye. A last pun, on Bianca's name, the Italian for 'white'.
being a winner An example of the faulty agreement still very prevalent today. 'As I am the winner, I can wish you good-night'.

Revision questions on Act V

1 Show how Lucentio's scheme and Tranio's devices lead up to a noisy scene for the entertainment of Petruchio and Katherina.

2 Kate's performance is a triumph for Petruchio, who has bet heavily on her. If acting her part, would you think of yourself as a changed woman motivated by awakened love, or only a shrew tamed against her will?

3 Contrast the Tranio in Scene 1 of this Act with the Tranio of Scene 2. Can you account for any differences?

Shakespeare's art in *The Taming of the Shrew*

Introduction

'Thou art not for an age but for all time.' (Ben Jonson)

Shakespeare achieved two firsts in our national literature, as poet and as playwright – something not claimed for any man of letters in any other nation. His plays have received worldwide recognition; his poetry is embedded in the dialogue of those plays. His powers of expression matched his genius in the creation of character. His lines, the best of which were poetically inspired, were composed for the utterance of professional actors entertaining audiences of varying tastes. He knew his fellow-actors and the roles they were best at undertaking. Through them as mouthpieces he was also at work on the minds of those who watched his dramas unfold, showing them human nature at its best and its worst, stimulating their imaginations by bringing old stories to life before their eyes and affording them opportunities to exercise their judgement between right and wrong, loyalty and treachery, love and hate, wisdom and folly. They beheld good and evil deeds, understood the motives and flinched at the consequences. All the world became a stage for spectators to behold sudden changes in circumstances, complete changes in character, and, particularly in this play, amusing changes of costume. Perhaps the subtlest 'change' of all would be that by which members of the audience identified themselves for a while with one or more of those they were watching.

For generations it has been argued that his marvellous inventions could not possibly be the work of a countryman come up to town; the mystery of his personality, on the other hand, reinforces the appeal of his creations. He was many-sided, with no bias, no doctrine to preach, no malice towards his contemporaries, no subservience to authority and no respect for mobs; he sculpted life from the beautiful to the grotesque, without sentiment or cynicism. What personal feelings he had – attractions to friends and emotional involvements with women – he expressed in a few poems and sonnets which cannot be positively said to be either based on real experience or written merely as literary exercises. In brief, Shakespeare was a poetical dramatist, not a poet who used the forms of drama, as did our second greatest poet, John Milton. It is the poetry that enriches his work away from the stage and endows his characters with the immortality of endless editions.

His greatness was acknowledged in his own day, and his works, while they fluctuated in public esteem during the following centuries, have never been more popular than over the past hundred years. Scholars in various parts of the world have devoted years, in some cases a lifetime, to wider and more intensive research into the texts, and to the discovery of fresh clues and new interpretations. In all but a few of his plays his imagination and wealth of diction have stirred the hearts of full houses – the voices may change, but the words are the same. The Old Vic Theatre took five years to present the entire series. None of his plays was written for the study; all had to come across the boards to that sea of faces on whose reception (handclaps or hisses) depended their success or failure. Least of all would their author have expected them to be a staple topic for generations of students taking examinations in English Literature. In the following commentary opinions are those formed or accepted by the editor; they are offered to the student as an aid to forming his own judgements and, it is hoped, to getting more enjoyment from the play.

Structure, setting, theme

Structure

Two plots run roughly parallel, one, by virtue of the characters and the incidents, being more important than the other. They double each other in similarities and create contrast by their differences. This pattern is typical of Shakespeare's construction: it was no rigid system, like the forms of classical drama; it served the main purpose of his work, the lifelike portrayal of character.

Both plots are concerned with wooings which lead to marriages. The ladies are sisters, but there the similarity ends: one is a duel, over the clear-cut issue of wifely obedience; the other is a competition among several suitors as to who shall be the husband. Petruchio probably disguises his real self and over-reacts against Kate's temper; Lucentio disguises his personal identity in his over-reaction to the beauty of Bianca. Petruchio starts out on marriage in terms of money and ends up as a perfect partner; Lucentio lives in a sentimental dream and ends up making a mean first bid on his wife's loyalty. The first couple are independent of their fathers: Petruchio's is dead and Kate's has wished her off onto the first-comer. The second couple unaccountably deceive their respective parents, pursuing a romantic elopement when there is no need for one.

Scenes from the two plots alternate almost systematically. In Act I Lucentio and Petruchio make their separate appearances in Padua. Act II is a long and involved single scene, in which Petruchio challenges Kate, and Tranio wins the 'auction' but requires a 'father'. In Act III the first scene is a quiet duel between the two tutors; the second is the wild wedding of Petruchio and Kate. Act IV balances Kate's ordeals with the shifty manoeuvres of her sister's admirers. Act V reaches a climax in the confrontation of the fathers, followed by the more subdued but more significant final scene in which the wager on the obedience of the three wives sets the seal on the triumph of Petruchio. But the wager would have been a lame affair without a third wife. Hence Hortensio is provided with a ready-made one, who has a touch of the shrewishness just shed by Kate.

The intertwining of the plots helps to speed up the play, each intervening scene making appear possible the swift passage of time between the one preceding it and the one following it. Even Lucentio's brief word with Tranio in III,2,136 is enough to make us forget, when Gremio comes back with his account of the wedding, that Petruchio has only just left the stage to *fetch* the bride-to-be. The duration of the action cannot be reckoned in hours – the playthings of Petruchio – and the lapse of days is only hinted at in Nathaniel's greeting 'Welcome home, Grumio.' The play is perhaps measured by moods: petulance, suspicion, impatience, jealousy, indignation – the whole 'gamut' of emotions.

The three descriptions of events off-stage, so economical of time and stage-production, are all the more sensational for having to be imagined: Biondello's account, in loving detail, of the bridegroom's appearance, Gremio's disapproving report of his behaviour in church, and Grumio's cryptic outline of what happened on the way home.

The stage was usually extended into the pit by an 'apron', allowing space for one group to observe another and comment on its actions: Lucentio's group watching Baptista's in I,1, Petruchio's overhearing Gremio's in I,2, and the standing aside of Petruchio and Kate to enjoy the fun of others' disagreements. There would be room for Lucentio and Biondello to hide behind some stage property, instead of leaving altogether, in the manoeuvres of IV,4 (as suggested in the textual notes). At the back of the stage was a recess between the two doors, which was curtained off when not required; used on occasion for interior scenes, it would serve in this play, with a window, as Lucentio's lodging, or with a door, for the three wives to withdraw into and return through. Above it was a balcony, used for defiance by a besieged garrison or for lovers' farewells. Thither Sly would be conveyed 'aloft', though some later producers prefer a corner of the stage proper, especially on account of the number of persons for whom space is needed: the lord and three serving-men, Sly's 'lady' and her attendants.

The most controversial feature in the structure of the play is the use of what came to be called the Induction. In the erratically divided Folio edition, *Actus Primus* includes this with the first two acts! These two introductory scenes are unique among Shakespeare's plays: perhaps it was an experiment he did not care to repeat. They may be the surviving part of a complete framework, as in the *other* and inferior play, *The Taming of a Shrew*, in which case the remainder might have been omitted by the editors if not actually taken out by the author himself, reducing the episode to an introduction only. What then would be its purpose, in part or as a whole? Several of Shakespeare's plots are set in Italy, but possibly this tale, set in one of the wealthiest parts of Europe, where the streets seethed with intrigue, schemers donned masks and disguises, love was a passionate pursuit as well as a commercial venture, conversation was full of airy persiflage and actions often wildly extravagant, needed a link with soberer English life. Not town life, but a rural setting, with the manor-house close by and the tinker collapsed outside the tavern.

Setting

Apart from the Induction, *The Taming of the Shrew* has a hard urban environment. Every scene is located either in the formal reception room of a house or on the pavement outside, with one exception – the road from Petruchio's house back to Padua – and there is nothing of the country about that. The only familiar Engish feature is the mud on the road.

The names of Italian cities mentioned are a roll-call of contemporary finance, commerce, arts and scholarship: Padua (Baptista and family), Pisa (Lucentio), Verona (Petruchio), Mantua (the Pedant), Florence (its university), Venice (finery), Genoa (an inn), Bergamo (Tranio's father). This leads us to wonder, as many have done, whether Shakespeare seized the opportunity, when the theatres were closed in 1593 because of plague, to travel abroad, particularly to Italy, where this and other comedies of his are set. No evidence has so far been discovered of such a visit – there is only the impression conveyed by details like the Italian words, the Italian pictures in Ind. 2, 50–61 and possibly the offering of hands in a match (II,1, 307–11). Petruchio and Hortensio greet each other like two old friends, in whole phrases as if they were real Italians on home territory. The most intriguing name is the one assumed by Lucentio when presenting himself as a tutor: *cambio* is still Italian for 'change' (anything from loose coins in one's pocket to stock-market quotations). This is not inappropriate in a part of the world which gave Lombard Street its name, though another impression of an ex-patriate Shakespeare might have been 'The pleasant garden of great Italy' (I,1,4). Tranio's bold exposition of his master's riches smacks fantastically of the wealth accumulated when Mediterranean trade was at its height.

There are also hints of inter-city competition, not always pacific (IV,2,81). To Lucentio his home town of Pisa seems a puddle in comparison with the oceanic proportions of Padua, whose famous university had thousands of students. The names of prominent men in one city were common knowledge in another. An obvious incongruity appears when Petruchio, who in I,2,100 declared he knew Baptista, approaches him in II,1,47 as a stranger, and is even asked his name and place of origin!

The characters, however, remain obstinately English for the most part, in dress, speech and custom. The luxurious country-house, to which the tinker is conveyed and where attempts are made to make him believe he is the owner thereof, provides more local colour than the rest of the play put together. In the words of the lord himself, aided and abetted by his serving-men, we see in imagination a well-drilled household, rich furniture and artistic tapestries, a stable full of horses, and hawks and hounds for hunting. There are physicians in attendance, and strolling players offer entertainment in the hall in return for accommodation. Other glimpses of contemporary life in England are of falcon-training, horse-equipment (worn-out), extravagance in feminine fashions, the roasting of chestnuts, bluffing at cards, lodging at inns (remembered long after!) and the 'banquet', that light course after the main meal, including fruit and wine, and taken in some great houses in specially built pavilions on the roof, whence views would be enjoyed over the formal gardens and the surrounding countryside.

Theme

It may be that in some quarters the less said about the theme the better! Some may indeed dismiss the conclusion as abject submission to male tyranny. Nothing, however, in Shakespeare's plays is so simple and clear-cut. The chief reward in studying this play is arriving at a true assessment of the two main characters, and on that no two critics are going to be in complete agreement. The student should seek to identify the better side of Petruchio and detect signs of a genuine, even affectionate reconciliation.

As again in Shakespeare, there is no single conclusion: less conspicuous than Katherina's new-found eloquence is the attitude of Bianca, who quietly demonstrates that subtlety achieves more than hysterics. A play devoted only to the contest between Petruchio and Katherina (or should it be Katherina and Petruchio?) would have been far too short for a full performance, so Shakespeare interwove with it the scenes concerning Bianca: they double the action, assist the passage of time and provide a contrast. They are inferior to those of the main plot, and some critics believe they are the work of someone else.

The play, therefore, is no blatant exercise in sex-discrimination, but rather a workmanlike blending of two popular pieces of fiction. They present two unusual examples of lovemaking: (1) wooing a wild-cat by atrocious ill-treatment masquerading as 'love', and (2) obtaining secret assignments in disguise that end in elopement. Which is the lesser of these two evils? To spectators both courses might seem unreasonable, but drama thrives on human eccentricities, even senseless contradiction. If the student has not yet found his own satisfactory 'theme', the following is seriously suggested: In the interests of civilization (and a quiet life) *the wild must be tamed.*

The characters

Petruchio

There is much of the Renaissance man in Petruchio's make-up. In love with life, beauty and what money can buy, he has started spending his inheritance on travel and is looking for a woman of wealth to be his wife. He is bold, boastful and ready with a wager. Having encountered dangers in pitched battles and violent storms, he is not to be cowed by a woman's tongue. For him a wealthy marriage means a happy one, until this rather mercenary approach, in which he actually agrees to the contract before he sets eye on his bride-to-be, gives place gradually to admiration, then to delight and finally to love. The Tamer of the Shrew is himself tuned to finer emotions in this duel of wills.

Of the same school as Benedick and Orlando, he is more than a masculine foil to the wit and charm of the opposite sex; it is he who leads, and Katherina who is driven to follow. Where Portia, Rosalind and Viola disguise themselves as men, here it is Petruchio who probably assumes a temperament at variance with his real disposition, which is good-humoured and generous. In a play with so many false identities, it is natural enough for the hero to adopt a character, both voluble and violent, with the express purpose of changing the nature and outlook of the self-willed girl he has impetuously offered to marry.

The act of 'taming' anybody or anything is not a gentle performance: it smacks of the whip, the repeated command and the final word of praise. This, with various refinements of Petruchio's invention, is what Katherina gets. But Petruchio is no brutal wife-batterer: he inflicts hardships and deprivations on her, but never does he raise a hand to strike. His confidence and persistence win the day, and when she ultimately and unreservedly submits, he has already given in to her personal charm, recognized by him under the mask of aggressiveness for which her life at home has no doubt been responsible.

The character of Petruchio is open to differing interpretations; he will certainly be anathema (the 'male chauvinist pig') to feminist champions! Some questions are not to be answered with certainty – after all, no stage character can be written down completely defined in every aspect. The conclusions of the last three paragraphs are open to challenge. One wonders how much of his performance is consciously acted and how much is natural to him. Is he merely asserting his masculine authority or genuinely seeking to influence Katherina's behaviour? Are his professions of doing everything in her own interest just adding insult to injury, or is there evidence of a real tender regard? He throws very little light on his motives in the two soliloquies, the one in which he reveals his plan to overwhelm her with contradictory praise, and the other which treats her as a wild thing to be made obedient by denial of food and sleep. He pushes his punishment on occasion to extremes, making fresh and illogical demands even after he has gained his point. When there is nothing more to be said, he says it! It is only at the end that we are aware of the attachment that has formed itself in his heart, yet even then he does not hesitate to humiliate her (in modern eyes) by a demonstration of her unswerving obedience to his slightest request. We may even suspect that his expression of admiration might have been uttered by a falconer delighted by the perfect display given by the hawk he has trained so rigorously! The essence of the matter is that the man of adventure who cheerfully gambled his success in marriage on a friend's report and gaily undertook to subdue a maiden with a sharp tongue, and performed 'wonders' in so doing, stands revealed as the husband in full control, who admires his wife – provided she obeys him.

Katherina

Katherina must be admitted to the select band of Shakespeare's heroines, if only by virtue of the sufferings she has to endure. At times the punishment seems excessive for the possession of a cutting tongue and a readiness to slap; she appears more offended against than offending; there is more Taming than Shrew. That, of course, is the stuff of entertainment, that is what the audience expects. In these encounters it is Petruchio's eloquence against her obstinacy. This is worn down more by his bold assertions and outrageous demands than by the physical hardships she has to go through. Whether bandying crude puns with her or paying her pretty compliments, defying potential enemies or pouring invective on those who displease him, his speeches echo round the stage; her utterances are far fewer, and during the course of the action become less shrill and more subdued in their protest.

The substance of the main plot consists of these recurring efforts by Kate to throw off the yoke he is imposing, each thwarted by his cunning. When the wedding feast is ready she makes the supreme challenge, as a bride kept waiting at the church-door, married in indecent haste and with riotous indecorum to a groom in disreputable attire, and now being hustled away before even a toast can be drunk. But Petruchio has merely to assert his marital rights and draw his sword in her 'defence' for this resistance to crumble.

One line from this wedding scene is significant. Petruchio says these words to Kate, as we must suppose, since there is unlikely to be other opposition:

Nay, look not big, nor stamp, nor stare, nor fret.

This suggests that much of her part is gesture rather than words (and therefore dependent on the personal interpretations of individual actresses). Nearly half of what she says is concentrated in the final speech. For a 'shrew', she is, apart from the long exchange of puns when she first meets Petruchio, singularly sparing of comment. What she says now is to the point, clear, idiomatic and indicative of both a sense of humour and emotional sensibility. It is a mature and contented Kate who, having shared with him the amusement provided by the crisis in the other love-affair, takes the initiative:

Husband, let's follow, to see the end of this ado.

And the Shrew is overtaken by modesty. Asked for a kiss, she protests:

What, in the midst of the street?

Listening to her 'epilogue', in which she enlarges on the labours undertaken and the dangers faced by the husband on the wife's behalf, we wonder wherever she 'studied all this goodly speech'!

Lucentio and Bianca

Like Petruchio, Lucentio is a visitor to Padua, but in the role of a student accompanied by a faithful and efficient servant, who is devoted to him and has been told by his young master's father to look well after him. Ambitious to recompense his father for his affection and generosity, he listens soberly to Tranio (who speaks almost as a *tutor* to his pupil) recommending a combination of dry philosophic study with the pleasanter perusal of love poems. The eyes of the bookish young student, his head full of amatory legends, are immediately fixed on Bianca; her demure looks and discreet words make him her instant and passionate lover. He compares her beauty to that of the mythical Europa who captivated Jove himself. His idealistic attitude to her is in direct contrast to the worldly bargaining with which Petruchio prefaces his wooing of Kate.

Unlike Petruchio, too, he reveals nothing in soliloquies, so we can only assume that his involved intrigues come from reading old romances with their tortuous plots. Having adopted the disguise of a schoolmaster, he replaces himself (in a strange city where he is unknown) with Tranio, and further requests this ingenious aide of his to offer himself as a fresh 'suitor' to Bianca, for reasons 'both good and weighty', which are never expressed, but are realized in two developments: (1) Gremio is discouraged and is outbid in offers of wealth for the hand of Bianca, and (2) the other suitor, Hortensio, is persuaded to join Tranio (whom he has been deluded into accepting as a rival called 'Lucentio') in renouncing Bianca after watching her flirtatious behaviour with 'Cambio' (the real Lucentio). Once brought together, the lovers leave everything to Tranio, who prepares his father-substitute to sign a marriage contract (actually for one between Bianca and him, Tranio!) and organizes their secret wedding by despatching Biondello to warn the local priest. After flitting like two shadows to a ceremony unseen, unheard and uncommented on, they steal back in time to save the others involved in Lucentio's schemes from dire punishment.

Just when harmony has been established between the wilder pair, this ingeniously contrived partnership is threatened with discord! And not just from the ruffled feelings of parents, who come to accept things with a good grace in the last scene, but in the more spirited behaviour of Bianca herself. Unaware of her husband's heavy betting on her instant obedience, she, no doubt continuing the playfulness which preceded her exit, as any 'household' wife might on receiving a similar summons, sends back the excuse that she is 'busy'. When she and the Widow are brought in by the triumphant Kate, Lucentio, with something of Petruchio's former mercenary outlook, reproaches her with costing him five (strictly, one) hundred crowns, and is answered:

The more fool you for laying on my duty.

The little shrew!

The suitors

Gremio is a wealthy old man who wishes to invest in a young wife; he professes a fervent love for her and is confident his riches will win her over. His admiration of her is paralleled by a fierce dislike of her sister, whom he insults by suggesting she should be 'carted' rather than 'courted', and by calling her openly 'this fiend of hell'. One reason for his anger is the interdict on further courting of Bianca until Kate is married. He immediately sets about finding a tutor for Bianca, while seeing little hope of a husband for Kate. He himself would sooner face a public flogging than endure her tongue. However, he is prepared to reward anyone found to undertake the task.

Hortensio, his younger rival, provides a link with the main plot in that he is already a friend of Petruchio, who calls on him immediately after his arrival in Padua. He seizes on Petruchio's declared intention of marrying well by telling him of a desirable match with but one snag – a sharp tongue. The consent of his friend, amazing as it is, tempts him to arrange his own under-cover courtship, disguised as one of the tutors sought by Baptista. His return, wounded over the head, from his encounter with Kate heightens the tension with which we see Petruchio await *his* first acquaintance with his Shrew. Tricked by Tranio into spying on Bianca, he speedily finds consolation by acquiring a wife (without even the mention anywhere of a wedding) and shares Lucentio's humiliation. Of the three ladies, one batters him, the second rejects him and the third loses him his wager: all of which does something to restore the balance of the sexes.

Gremio, after losing an auction in which he has bid his entire wealth, is further shocked by the farcical wedding of Kate and finally stunned by the revelation of the runaway marriage of the lady of his choice with a stranger, none other than the hired tutor in whom he put his trust. All that is now left him is a share in the feast when Bianca is married.

This sub-plot of Bianca's suitors, four in all, is involved and marked by discrepancies, but we should remember Shakespeare went to work with a quill pen and not a computer; also its patchiness suggests that he was hastily piecing together a lively performance that required little imaginative thought. Evidence of this may be found in the 'Widow' and the 'Pedant', the only characters in all his comedies with more than a walking-on part who have not been given personal names, and that in a play where Petruchio's lengthy retinue have all been christened, including three who do not even appear. It is less likely that these were stock parts – the merry widow and the elderly schoolmaster – than that in the haste of composing the dialogue and getting the play produced, Shakespeare did not find time to decide on their names. Perhaps he left it to his 'collaborator', regarded by some critics as responsible for much of the sub-plot; if the last lines of the play are this man's, then he was an unreliable hack.

The old men

In a play featuring large sums in dowries and wagers the owners of wealth are prominent, and these are men advanced in years, with the exception of Petruchio. *Baptista* is rich enough to make a stake of a hundred crowns look paltry beside the twenty thousand he adds to it. Having no son, he is attached to his younger daughter, though, rather in the fashion of Shakespeare's day, his concern with her marrige shows scant regard for her personal feelings. This may explain her readiness to join in conspiring to deceive him. He also respects convention when he requires the elder one to be married first, though the suggestion has been made, with nothing to support it, that he finds Kate's pricing of herself out of the marriage market a useful means of postponing the departure of his beloved Bianca. Again, in common with 16th-century tastes, he sees nothing wrong in accepting the courtship of her by Gremio, a man of about his own age. Prizing his favourite daughter highly in terms of worldly goods, he promises her to the champion whose knightly 'deeds' in the form of rich furnishings, livestock and merchant fleets exceed those of his adversary! Anyone is welcome to Kate (an offer made in the open street); her tongue has often given him a rough ride.

Baptista does not hide the prospective trouble in front of one who courts Kate, and his words of warning are reinforced by the appearance of a bandaged Hortensio. Meeting Kate after her first encounter with Petruchio, he is struck by her subdued manner, which however vanishes when she rounds on him for marrying her off to a 'ruffian'. Nevertheless, he blesses the match, and when they are gone, confesses to having gambled, like a trader risking a fortune. The profit he hopes for is a state of peace in his household.

Another old man, of respectable appearance and paternal mien, merchant or schoolmaster (according to Biondello, but two occupations distinctly incompatible today) is the anonymous

Pedant (a professional schoolmaster in Shakespeare's day, and not one fond of displaying his learning). Engaged in some unpedagogic business, peddling some bills of exchange (was he a merchant joining in the prevailing game of disguises?), he is scared into acting the part of a man he has never seen; he pleases Baptista by his unpedantic 'plainness' and 'shortness' as he 'fathers' Tranio disguised as 'Lucentio'.

He is so carried away by his successful impersonation and by the conviviality at the signing of the contract that, when the real Vincentio arrives, he addresses him brazenly through the window and treats him as a criminal impostor who must be arrested. He calls him a 'madman' and stoutly maintains that 'Lucentio' is his heir. This persistence in what he knows to be downright deception may be explained by the assumption that Vincentio is far away, or by a fear of being unmasked as a Mantuan and therefore an enemy, one liable to arrest.

At the height of the dispute one old man, Baptista, taken in by the imposture of another old man, the Pedant, is ordering the arrest of a third old man, father of the young man who, unknown to him, has just married his daughter. While Baptista is merely deceived, the unfortunate *Vincentio* is subjected to far more than deception: first greeted in very strange fashion, then impersonated, suspected by his new acquaintance, denied recognition by those to whom he pays wages, insulted and finally threatened with arrest. So shaken is Vincentio that he expresses astonishment to see his son alive. At the banquet he is content to be a spectator of the extraordinary demonstration of marital harmony by the two young people whose first greeting was a piece of mockery.

In the wide gallery of Shakespeare's characters the elderly form a considerable band, as various in individual traits as any other age-group. They range from those whose years of experience invest them with a special dignity, like Prospero and Gaunt, to talkative senior citizens, like Polonius, Gonzalo and Justice Shallow. There is the tragedy of authority impaired by old age in King Lear and the comedy of old age impaired by drink in Falstaff and Toby Belch. Frequently we meet an 'Old Man' who is weatherwise or possesses local knowledge of people and places. Their weaknesses, characteristic of their age, are a fixity of ideas, pride of family, a peevish assertion of authority, a readiness to impart their wisdom, or sheer garrulity. In *The Taming of the Shrew*, while Petruchio is engaged in reducing Katherina to desperation, the rest of the action is based on the deception of the respective fathers of Lucentio and Bianca, which includes an act of imposture which the third old man is forced to commit; there is, too, a fourth in Gremio, the elderly suitor who, in spite of keeping a sharp look-out for any double-dealing, is himself completely hoodwinked!

The servants

While this elder generation seems able to manage by itself when abroad, it is the young gallants who are attended by one or more personal servants. This may reflect contemporary custom – indulgent parents equipping their sons with suitable retinues of followers on their travels – but the chief functions of the servants here, as in other plays, are to provide light relief by jesting, to discuss plans with their masters for the benefit of the audience, and, on occasion, to make mistakes, in addition to their usual employment in carrying messages or introducing visitors. The three with whom we are concerned have all an independence of spirit, even an impudent familiarity which may well point to a camaraderie between master and man in Shakespeare's day which largely disappeared in a later world of 'Upstairs, Downstairs'.

Tranio is as much a companion as a valet; he has been given what almost amounts to guardianship over an unpredictable young romantic so ardent in pursuit of fantasy that he has failed to keep in touch with his father for some time. While the entranced Lucentio can think of little else but gazing on Bianca's beauty, Tranio is left to carry out his elaborate instructions and even to add to them. He contributes to the tutoring (1) the lute for 'Licio' who has thoughtlessly come thus unprovided, and (2) classical texts with Lucentio's name on them for 'Cambio'. He is quick-witted, with a ready tongue; he quotes Latin or makes classical allusions; his first two words are in Italian. He puts on the airs and graces of a young man of fashion and dispenses hospitality as if born to it. He makes eloquent speeches, presents himself as a convincing suitor and unblushingly piles up offers of wealth that cause Gremio, a man of genuine wealth, to give up in despair, though not without some suspicion.

The last act in Tranio's double existence is to defy Gremio to say he is not Lucentio. With the appearance of the real Lucentio, his whole edifice of pretence (no doubt thoroughly enjoyed) collapses, and he vanishes in the direction of the domestic offices to reappear, in the final scene of the banquet, like some

Admirable Crichton, back in service and carrying in the dishes.

His junior is the ubiquitous page-boy, *Biondello*, given to cheeky utterances. Having loitered behind at the start of the play, he is taken aback by the exchange of hat and coat between Lucentio and Tranio, and is then strictly enjoined not to give away these assumed identities. This must have become a fixed idea in his flighty mind, for, after recognizing a very inexact 'resemblance' to Vincentio in the Pedant, he then refuses, with outrageous flippancy, to acknowledge the head of the family in which he serves. For this he is beaten and flees to bring Lucentio to put things right. What happens between Vincentio and his two disloyal servants remains a secret, but Biondello has one more part to play, for which he is by temperament well suited: to skip in and out as messenger, bringing back the ladies' pert answers to their husbands' requests.

But his most extraordinary performance is his detailed description of Petruchio and his horse and man arriving for the wedding. With its torrent of technical terms, this turns Biondello into a stable-boy who has swallowed the vet's dictionary of equine diseases, and would come more aptly from Grumio, who presumably had saddled his master's steed and knew just what he himself was wearing.

Grumio has even more of the clown about him (the nearness of his name to Gremio is confusing, and further evidence of the tendency in this play to carelessness over names). He is loyal to his master, but not blind to his faults. He has the boldness of the jester, and worries at a phrase like 'knock me here' with the pertinacity of a dog with a bone. He comments freely on Petruchio's apparent obsession with money, on Katherina's shrewishness, on Hortensio's scheming; he is sarcastic about Gremio's age and his wealth, but is ready to wager that his master, who fears nobody, will be the winner over Kate. His small stature does not save him from Petruchio's anger on two occasions. At the wedding he follows him without a word: we forget he is there, until he is told to draw his sword in 'defence' of his new mistress. In view of Kate's kindness shown to him on the journey, it is a mean little game he plays with her, offering food and then withholding it. In the next scene he is engaged in a farcical duel of words with the tailor. After this exhausting contest, he has nothing further to say, not even at the banquet.

Sly

A paragraph must suffice for one who spends most of his time on the stage in a drunken stupor or fast asleep; yet Christopher Sly is a part that has been taken by some of our best comic actors, and he rates a mention in universal encyclopedias. His brief appearance has an earthy reality; he is more than mere clown, but not witty enough for a jester. He is the public-bar transferred to the stateroom. In a play of false identities consciously assumed to deceive others, he is the victim of deception in having a false identity, with much circumstantial evidence, thrust upon him. He cannot reason himself out of his luxurious surroundings. He was probably copied from a living model in a Warwickshire village; with his foreign tags and his boasted ancestry he may have been a caricature of someone known personally to the dramatist. It is difficult to persuade him that he is a long-deranged lord who has just recovered his wits; he is more convinced by the luxury of the furnishings than by the opportunities offered him to enjoy the best in art and sport. It is therefore hardly surprising that the long and involved opening scene bores him; even if he remained awake in the scenes that follow, it is also highly improbable that he would draw any kind of comparison between the 'wife' sitting demurely at his side and the fiery Katherina presented for his edification. The tinker disappears in the darkness unredeemed; it is the Shrew whose fate it is to be transformed.

Style

There is little of the excessive ornament of the early plays of Shakespeare, and less of the close-packed expression of the later ones. The dialogue is directly concerned with the motives, plans and actions of the characters. A fair number of literary allusions and some word-play would appeal to subtle-minded lawyers in the galleries; the knock-about incidents and risqué jokes would delight the illiterate groundlings in the pit. There are fewer sustained speeches than usual, and only one of any length – Kate's concluding homily. The speed of the action, the number of persons involved in the average scene, and the somewhat closed circle of courting, dowries, marriages and wedding feasts leave no room for serious reflection, emotional sentiments or imaginative moralizing. Petruchio's two soliloquies are to state what he is going to do, what he has done and what he is still prepared to do. The only concession to the imagination is the extended metaphor of the falcon-training; Bianca, too, does not escape a sporting reference – she is 'mewed up' by her father and dismissed as an erring 'haggard' by the disillusioned Hortensio. Almost the only simile, apart from the far-fetched ones in Kate's speech, is Petruchio's half-mocking defence of the old clothes he proposes they should visit her home in:

And as the sun breaks through the darkest clouds
So honour peereth in the meanest habit.

He also uses one of the few metaphors to mark his victory over Kate's temperament:

Thus the bowl should run against the bias.

There are a few comparisons with nature, analogies from bird and reptile fashions (IV,3) and a smattering of proverbial sayings: Gremio's unromantic observation, 'our cake's dough on both sides' is soon matched by that of Hortensio, 'there's small choice in rotten apples' (I,1,108,134). The rest is mostly puns, including one on Kate's own name (the wild cat of II,1,270). Her first encounter with Petruchio is largely the thrust and parry of a whole con*cat*enation of such puns: move, bear, bee, buzz, sting, tail, arms, cock's comb, sour, crab-apple. Other examples are given under *Literary Terms*.

In a play involving tutors and a pedant some sprinkling of classical allusions is to be expected, but, in view of the plot, they are mostly legendary love affairs: Dido, Europa, Helen of Troy, Diana, Lucretia. The latter half is quite devoid of such mythical figures, who could only add to the complexity of actual personalities; and they could have no place in the disciplined state of domestic bliss portrayed in Katherina's confession of faith – unless in tapestry form on the walls of a stateroom!

The only accepted quotations to come out of the play are Tranio's advice on reading:

No profit grows where is no pleasure ta'en:
In brief, sir, study what you most affect.

and Kate's ironical remark to her father:

You have showed a tender fatherly regard
To wish me wed to one half lunatic.

The bareness of this play's diction shows by comparison how much Shakespeare's poetic imagination enriched his greater comedies.

Verse and prose

The bulk of Shakespeare's dramatic works are composed in blank verse (iambic pentameter unrhymed), though most of his plays, certainly all his comedies, have passages of prose dialogue throughout. This difference in tone and emotional impact was used to distinguish the speech of characters of social or political importance from that of humbler people or comics. A further distinction was made between speeches by the same character in differing circumstances or varying moods, for example, verse for formal harangues or passionate appeals, prose for practical arrangements or jesting. In our play there is constant interchange of verse and prose, a sign of the author's maturer method of expression; for instance, Grumio's comments, in prose, are inserted between the blank verse speeches of the others. It is possible to make too much of this contrast, especially in comedy. Shakespeare must have written verse with the same facility as prose, and could slip easily from one to the other.

The use of rhyme, chiefly in couplets, happened as it occurred to him, without adding any significance to the lines affected. A single rhyming couplet at the end of a scene clinched it like the lowering of a modern curtain: on the Elizabethan stage the actors had to walk off.

Petruchio's verbal duel with Kate in II,1 includes some *stichomythia*, dialogue conducted in single alternating lines, from examples in classical drama. The opponents in the argument seize in turn on a point made in the preceding line. Shakespeare is possibly making conscious use of this device in ll,198–243, where the tension is heightened by the metrical rhythm, but he characteristically broke up some of the lines into something more natural.

Vocabulary

In the course of some centuries many of Shakespeare's words (and his was the largest vocabulary of all English writers) have become obsolete; even more of a problem are the large number still in use which had a different meaning in those days or which have lost the particular meaning attached to them when he wrote them down. Words, like clothes, are subject to changes of fashion; they go out of use with the objects they were names for, or are adapted to new inventions or practices. Besides the change-over in everyday matters, many words survived in separate use as 'poetic' terms; others were then and still are employed on special occasions because of their antique flavour (archaisms); a distressingly large number have become debased by coarse associations.

Among human attributes, 'cunning' meant 'skill', while 'skills not' equalled 'does not matter'; an 'invention' was an *idea* thought up; the 'stomach' was the seat of courage or just inclination; 'humour' was still a disposition, optimistic or pessimistic, placid or bad-tempered, according to the blend of the four bodily 'humours', while 'pleasant' was 'humorous'. This was a world of 'good sooth' and 'I trow', of links and kennels, of lutes and rush candles, of tapestries and three-legged stools, of bucklers and gawds, of argosies and their profitable 'traffic', of jades in harness and hungry falcons. Shakespeare drew from his vast store of words and used them,

According to the fashion and the time (IV,3,95).

General questions

1 What were Petruchio's methods of dealing with a 'shrew'? Show, by reference to three different occasions, how he carried them out.

Outline of points to cover in your answer:

(Introductory) Petruchio no professional shrew-tamer – in his travels hopes to meet a wife with a fortune (to add to his own) – is told by a friend of a young and beautiful heiress whose only fault is a scolding tongue – sees this as a challenge and apparently improvises the means by which to overcome her bad temper – morally supported in his decision to win her in marriage by the knowledge that his conquest would facilitate his friend's courtship of the sister.

(Method) Twice he announces his tactics beforehand in a soliloquy (a) before he sees her, the plan being to describe her outbursts as sweet and charming, (b) after leading her into the bridal chamber, when he explains his intention to 'train' her to obey him by starving her and depriving her of sleep – all in the name of the fondest love. The technique throughout is contradiction, and the opposition of violent temper and selfish conduct with behaviour which is far more extreme. (Three occasions) The following show successive stages in the treatment (1) *The wooing* Having boasted that a mere woman's tongue cannot daunt one experienced in storms and loud explosions he fights a wordy duel with Katherina in which no feelings are spared – at the end declares she is the very *opposite of reports* and praises her for virtues she clearly does not seem to possess (and well she knows it) – the only hint of physical violence is the threat to return a blow (which she does not provoke). The most dramatic part of this pattern of contradiction is his bold pretence of a secret agreement – this indeed may have a psychologically disarming effect on her. (2) *The wedding* Now it is deeds rather than words – Petruchio adopts the *opposite for himself* of what a young woman in her social position might expect: disreputable in appearance, he shows disrespect all round and exerts his violence on others – following irrational statements we now have unreasonable actions, in fact behaviour so extraordinary that it is more readily described than represented on stage.

(3) *The bridegroom's reception* Of the two scenes in Petruchio's house, both devoted to the steady torment of Katherina, the second has more significance: after the physical hardships of the journey, the lack of comfort, of food and of sleep, Katherina is now faced by the final battle of wills, over the choice of what to wear. Not only does he reject what she likes, he praises her for '*not*' liking it. The 'wild falcon' having been starved and berated into a measure of submission, – during the quarrel between Grumio and the tailor she has nothing to say – he starts to moralize

'tis the mind that makes the body rich

and descends to contradict her over trivialities

It shall be what o'clock I say it is

meanly accusing her of doing the contradicting.

(Conclusion) Katherina, however miserable, is never entirely a tool in his hands – throughout she retains enough spirit to make her a worthy mate to a masterful husband.

NB Avoid digressions into or references to *other* scenes; add suitable brief quotations.

2 Describe the three impersonations and state clearly the purpose with which each was undertaken.

3 Explain the parts of (a) Tranio, and (b) Hortensio, commenting on any discrepancies you notice.

4 For which of the older generation do you feel most sympathy and for which the least? Give your reasons.

5 Contrast the characters of the two sisters (a) at the beginning of the play, and (b) at the end.

6 Do you consider the omission of a conclusion to the Induction a structural weakness?

7 Distinguish among the various 'suitors' to Bianca with regard to motive and result.

8 Two arrivals in Padua prove to be fortunate and one unfortunate. Show briefly the effect of each on events in the play.

9 How many different kinds of verbal conflict between two persons take place? Explain what gave rise to each.

10 'The taming school'. How far do you think this expression, used in the sub-plot, is an apt description of what happens in the main plot?

11 Choose three incidents which you found most amusing and explain the situation in each case.
12 What differences do you notice between an Elizabethan wedding and a modern one?
13 Attempt the description of the interior of an Elizabethan mansion from details supplied in the play.
14 If you were the producer, would you choose a bare stage like that in Shakespeare's day, or one with scenery and adequate furniture? Justify your choice from your reading of the play.

Further reading

A Shakespeare Encyclopaedia, ed. O. J. Campbell and E. G. Quinn (Methuen 1966).

Everyman's Companion to Shakespeare, G. & B. Lloyd Evans (Dent 1978).

William Shakespeare, E. K. Chambers (OUP 1930).

Shakespeare (English Men of Letters), Sir Walter Raleigh (Macmillan 1907).

Shakespeare and his World, F. E. Halliday (Thames & Hudson 1956).

Introducing Shakespeare, G. B. Harrison (Penguin 1939).

William Shakespeare: the Early Comedies, D. Traversi (Chatto & Windus) 1960.

Any large central library will have (for reference) a copy in reduced fascimile of the First Folio.

Pan study aids Selected titles published in the Brodie's Notes series

Jane Austen Emma Mansfield Park Northanger Abbey Persuasion Pride and Prejudice

Geoffrey Chaucer (parallel texts editions) The Franklin's Tale The Knight's Tale The Miller's Tale The Nun's Priest's Tale The Pardoner's Tale Prologue to the Canterbury Tales The Wife of Bath's Tale

Joseph Conrad The Nigger of the Narcissus & Youth The Secret Agent

Charles Dickens Bleak House David Copperfield Dombey and Son Great Expectations Hard Times Little Dorrit Oliver Twist Our Mutual Friend A Tale of Two Cities

George Eliot Middlemarch The Mill on the Floss Silas Marner

E. M. Forster Howards End A Passage to India Where Angels Fear to Tread

William Golding Lord of the Flies The Spire

Graham Greene Brighton Rock The Power and the Glory The Quiet American

Thomas Hardy Chosen Poems of Thomas Hardy Far from the Madding Crowd Jude the Obscure The Mayor of Casterbridge Return of the Native Tess of the d'Urbervilles The Trumpet-Major

L. P. Hartley The Go-Between The Shrimp and the Anemone

Laurie Lee As I Walked Out One Midsummer Morning Cider with Rosie

Christopher Marlowe Doctor Faustus Edward the Second

John Milton A Choice of Milton's Verse Comus and Samson Agonistes Paradise Lost I, II

Sean O'Casey Juno and the Paycock The Shadow of a Gunman and the Plough and the Stars

George Orwell Animal Farm 1984

William Shakespeare Antony and Cleopatra As You Like It Coriolanus Hamlet Henry IV (Part 1) Henry IV (Part 2) Henry V Julius Caesar King Lear Love's Labour's Lost Macbeth Measure for Measure The Merchant of Venice A Midsummer Night's Dream Much Ado about Nothing Othello Richard II Richard III Romeo and Juliet The Sonnets The Taming of the Shrew The Tempest Twelfth Night The Winter's Tale